WITHDRAWN

FROM

WALKER MANAGEMENT LIBRARY

**Political
Violence**
and
**Civil
Disobedience**

Political
Violence
and
Civil
Disobedience

Ernest van den Haag

HARPER TORCHBOOKS ❦

Harper & Row, Publishers

New York, Evanston, San Francisco, London

POLITICAL VIOLENCE AND CIVIL DISOBEDIENCE

First TORCHBOOK edition published 1972.

LIBRARY OF CONGRESS CATALOG CARD NUMBER: 72–190092

STANDARD BOOK NUMBER: 06–131626–1

Designed by Yvette A. Vogel

CONTENTS

A NOTE ON NOTES

Notes have a bad reputation. They suggest tiresome trivia, erudite pedantries and obscure polemics or (at best) references of interest mainly to dedicated specialists. If the matter is worth discussing, why not in the text?

All too often there are enticing but collateral arguments to address, objections to refute, misunderstandings to ward off; and there are interesting applications and elaborations. Yet, if one allowed oneself to be seduced by such matters, the text would become diffuse and unmanageable. The main theme gains by straightforward presentation without strolls into fascinating byways, and by omission of baroque ornamentation, however dramatic.

To develop the argument in the most lucid and transparent, in the most austere and monodic way possible, is to forgo whatever is not strictly pertinent. Yet, the human mind is, fortunately, polyphonic, and responsive to the contrapuntal. I feel frustrated when I have no chance to explain why I disregarded what I disregarded, why I think some idea wrong, or although interesting or correct, not quite pertinent to the argument.

That is why I like notes. They let me stick to the internal logic of the argument and yet allow me to lure venturesome readers into exploration of the adjacent intellectual landscape—from which sometimes they can see the main road at a more interesting angle. Such excursions enrich the intellectual journey—unless you are in a great hurry; in which case you can omit the notes.

The ideal reader does not need the incidental information provided by the notes. But he is, alas, a mental construct—although I write for this homogeneous abstraction, as does every author. Actual readers are a heterogeneous lot. Some know about the concept of "natural law" and do not need an explanatory note. Others have vague or wrong notions. Without the explanatory note, the textual reference to "natural law" is unintelligible or misleading to them. Again, one reader may have been over-impressed with the relevance of Arrow's arguments on majority decisions (the note appended may disabuse him); another reader may realize that, whatever their merit, Arrow's arguments are not logically relevant to civil disobedience. (He can safely omit the note); still another reader has never heard of Arrow's arguments (the note dealing with them may lead him to pick up incidentally a very important notion).

The notes are provided, then, so that actual readers may supplement the text according to their actual needs. The ideal reader —if he's around anywhere—is not harmed; the actual reader may be helped. Looking right and left as well as straight ahead, makes life interesting for myself and argument—ultimately a reflection on life—more lively. I enjoy leisurely travel and exploration even of blind alleys: how else will I learn that they lead nowhere? But, fearing to lose my way, or my reader, I have made these excursions optional by confining them to notes. I hope I will have company.

P.S.   Short notes and reference notes identified by an asterisk are found at the bottom of the page to which they refer. Longer notes are numbered. At the bottom of the page the subject is indicated, and the reader is referred to the page on which to find the note.

Civil
Disobedience

Characterization

Public disobedience to government authority has become known as "civil disobedience"[1] when laws are defied for the sake of moral principle.

The laws or practices challenged need not be those disobeyed: the draft laws may be opposed by disobeying trespassing laws.[2] However, the disobedience must be visibly related to the matters protested and consistent with the moral principles to be vindicated. Ideally, civil disobedience involves injury to no one; and certainly harm to innocent bystanders, and even to those held responsible for whatever is opposed, and must remain minor. Civil disobedience differs from insurrection and from revolution by self-imposed restrictions such as these.

Strictly and legally speaking, one cannot publicly disobey a law and also publicly contend that one is "not guilty" of disobeying it. However, their acts are usually regarded as civil disobedience, if defendants plead "not guilty" to proclaim their *moral* guiltlessness, and to get a chance to denounce the law they admit they actually disobeyed. Even if the law which they publicly disobeyed on moral grounds is later held not to have been legally valid, their defiance still may be regarded as civil disobedience,

1. Disobedience, mutiny, and insubordination defined (p. 107).
2. Fortas's definition (p. 107).

because the challengers, though they do escape punishment, were willing to suffer it.[3]

Proponents of civil disobedience traditionally do not use force themselves—at least not against persons—although they may invite it. To exhibit the suasive character of their acts they do not resist enforcement of the laws they disobey by either fighting, or fleeing; they are willing to stand trial, and to suffer punishment. Thus they underline the public and symbolic, as well as the civic (civil) character of their conduct: they disobey civilly, as citizens (*cives*) who, except for the specific matters protested, feel bound to obey the laws.[4] Further, since they are usually weaker than the supporters of the opposed law, violence would not be effective.

Civil disobedience by definition is always regarded as unlawful at some point. Else it could not qualify as "disobedience." But the essential problem transcends all narrowly legal contentions: when, if ever, is there a *moral* right, or duty, to disobey a valid law or a lawful authority?[5] This philosophical problem is involved also in conscientious objection, a less extensive challenge to lawful authority, and in revolution, a more extensive one. Although the line is often blurred, civil disobedience can be distinguished from both.

Conscientious Objection

Conscientious objectors demand exemption from a legal obligation repugnant to their conscience. They disobey the law only if the privilege they seek is not granted. They need not resist the

3. On lawful and unlawful disobedience (p. 107).
4. Howard Zinn on submitting to punishment (p. 107).
5. On Obligation (p. 108).

legal obligation of those whose consciences permit them to comply or demand that laws be changed for everybody. In contrast, civil disobedience always demands not a special dispensation from, but a general change of, laws or policies: e.g., not exemption from, but abolition of the draft. And civil disobedience must be (putatively) unlawful, since disobedience to laws is used as a means of changing them (even though *post facto* the disobedience may be declared legal and the "law" invalid).

Conscientious objectors to military service are granted exemption in the U.S. if the conscientiousness of the objection is recognized—if the objector can show that his objection rests on general moral principles strongly and deeply held. For example, it is one thing to renounce war as a means to anything, another to spurn only a particular war—just as it is one thing to repudiate the death penalty in principle, and another to oppose inflicting it on a particular defendant. Motivation may well be moral in both instances.* But the conscience which only objects to some wars, or death sentences, depends on judgments of specific facts; whereas the conscience opposed, on principle, to all wars, regardless of circumstances, or to the death penalty, does not. The objector's judgment of specific facts (is *this* defendant actually guilty? Is *this* war necessary, useful, or just?) could not be allowed to prevail over that of courts and governments, without reducing their judgments to an opinion no more authoritative and enforceable than his.** (How useful a person who strongly opposes a particular war is in fighting it, is a different question; but certainly a prudential question and neither a legal nor a moral one.)

---

* This must be the reason which leads the American Civil Liberties Union *et al.* to defend conscientious objection to particular wars.

** For Ronald Dworkin's contrary views see Appendix B (p. 35).

Revolution

Whereas the ends of conscientious objection do not go as far as those of civil disobedience, the ends of revolution go beyond; so do the means. Civil disobedience is intended in the main to persuade by symbolic acts[6] and certainly to defy laws only so as to press for limited specific changes within the legal and political system. Revolution, however, is intended to change the whole political system; and, as a minimum, to coerce unpersuaded opponents, by whatever force is needed, so as to overthrow the government and to gain power for the revolutionaries.

Unsuccessful civil disobedience differs only in intent (and legal status) from conscientious objection, while successful civil disobedience, if it becomes extensive and ambitious enough, may develop into revolution, with, or without, violence.

History, Literature and Movements

Sophocles' tragedy *Antigone* is the *locus classicus* of civil disobedience. Creon, ruler of Thebes, orders proper burial for one of Antigone's brothers, who fell defending the city, while the other, who died attacking the city, was to be left "unwept, un-

6. Speaking and acting (p. 109).

tombed . . . for the hungry birds" and thus "robbed of his re-
lease." Antigone, defying Creon, commits "the crime of piety" by
burying her brother according to "the gods' unwritten and un-
failing laws" (against the advice of her sister Ismene who "can
not act against the citizens"). Creon sentences Antigone to death
despite the plea of his son who was to marry her. The chorus is
uneasy about the whole matter and the seer Teiresias warns of
divine punishment. But when Creon seeks to revoke the sentence,
he finds that Antigone, his son, and finally his wife have committed suicide. He withdraws disgraced. Whatever his power,
Sophocles suggests, no ruler has the right to demand acts or
omissions contrary to divinely ordained norms, such as those of
familial piety.

Socrates, as depicted by Plato in the *Apologia* and in *Crito,*
articulately dramatizes the perennial conflict between individual
conscience and social authority. Accused of corrupting the young
with atheistic ideas, Socrates pleads innocent. But he goes on to
say that, should the court find his discourses unlawful, he would
nevertheless continue them, since he felt an inescapable moral
duty to do so. Thus Socrates declared that he had not disobeyed
the law, but would do so, if the court should hold the law to
prohibit his conduct. He proposed civil disobedience if the law
were to prohibit what he thought it his duty to do—but he
pleaded "not guilty" to the actual charge of which he was convicted.

When he is sentenced to death Crito urges him to escape. But
Socrates refuses. He does not repudiate the laws and procedures
which still bind him in general as a citizen, even though he must
disobey when they prohibit—but only when they do—performance
of moral duties imposed by what the Christian tradition later will
call conscience. It is his moral duty, therefore, to submit to the
sentence pronounced according to law, as it was and remains his
moral duty to do what led to it. Socrates' view is shared by all
who believe that, on specific occasions, their own moral principles

may force them to disobey a social authority, or a specific rule, while yet they recognize the authority and its rulemaking prerogative as legitimate and, therefore, generally binding.

Legal theory often has postulated "a true law . . . which, in accordance with nature, applies to all men" (Cicero) and, discovered by (or identical with) *recta ratio* (right reason), is prior and superior to the laws of any ruler. St. Augustine already thought that "an unjust law is not a law" and Cicero wrote that no social authority "can absolve us from our obligation to obey this [natural] law." Neither, however, explicitly left it to individuals to decide when to disobey the government's law. Many Christian (and post-Christian) thinkers as well thought the laws of a ruler (positive laws) invalid "perversions of law rather than laws" (Thomas Aquinas) when in conflict with "natural" or "divine" laws. Accordingly, early Christians disobeyed Roman laws inconsistent with their beliefs, and later Christians on many occasions acted analogously. St. Thomas More reportedly was executed (1535) proclaiming himself "the king's good servant, but God's first."

"Natural" or "divine" law may require rulers to make positive laws prohibiting individual decisions (e.g., about abortion) or permitting them. Natural law also may justify individual decisions to obey social commands and institutions (such as slavery), or to disobey them. The decision depends on whether one thinks that "right reason" shows natural law to be on the side of the positive legislation or institution, or requires disobeying it. In either case an appeal is made to authority presumed higher than society, the ruler, or the individual's desire. But different people may interpret edicts of this higher authority differently. Psychoanalysis would locate this authority in the superego. In the past it was thought to be articulated by the church, and found in revelation or nature generally, or in human nature in particular.*

Most of the scholastics stressed the individual's duty to obey

---

* See footnote 14 on "natural law" (p. 115).

authority more than his duty to disobey. In the seventeenth century Thomas Hobbes went further in identifying justice with the sovereign's right to legislate. Since "the laws are the rules of just and unjust" he declared that "no law can be unjust." However, John Locke and David Hume discerned once more that individual claims could not be so completely surrendered as to exclude resistance when the sovereign abused his power. Both, however, appear to think of revolution more than of civil disobedience; and neither was able to preclude different interpretations, or abuses, of the term "abuse."

In modern times, particularly in America, Henry David Thoreau's passionate and eloquent lecture *On the Relation of the Individual to the State* (1848) has inspired many people to resist "unjust laws." The lecture, first published (as *Resistance to Civil Government*) in 1849, does not mention "civil disobedience" and received that title only in a posthumous edition. Nonetheless Thoreau named, although he did not father, civil disobedience. His own attitude seems generally antinomian, if not consistently so.

In his lecture Thoreau asserts that "the only obligation which I have a right to assume is to do at any time what I think right." Taken literally this is a truism: one does not do anything unless in some sense, one thinks it "right." But Thoreau meant to deny that "the citizen must . . . in the least degree resign his conscience to the legislator," i.e., he denied the morally obligatory character of law. (Somewhat surprisingly, Thoreau goes on to invite citizens to "break the law" only when "it requires you to be the agent of injustice to another.") However, Thoreau does not coherently discuss the occasions and limits of civil obedience, or disobedience, the likely, or desired, effects of either, nor, finally, the means of resistance to law. He intended disobedience to be persuasive; but he did not explicitly reject violence and later on he supported John Brown's bloody antislavery raid.

Mohandas K. Gandhi was deeply influenced by the aged Leo Tolstoi, who passionately rejected all violence. He won his first campaign of "passive resistance" in 1913, in South Africa, when the government of Ian Smuts yielded to the (antidiscrimination) demands of the local Indian community. Returning to India, Gandhi used his technique of nonviolent disobedience to law—which he extended and renamed "truth force"—to win a strike of textile workers (1918) and, later, some degree of desegregation for untouchables. Apart from cheerfully suffering the punishment imposed by the laws he disobeyed, Gandhi also morally black-mailed those he wished to influence, by fasting until his demands were met.[7] Gandhi finally achieved a peaceful transfer of English power to an independent Indian government. (Although relying on the techniques of civil disobedience, Gandhi obviously went beyond in his aims, though not in the means he urged.)

Gandhi's techniques of nonviolent disobedience have deeply influenced all such efforts (although outside India fasting was seldom used) and particularly those of the Rev. Martin Luther King, Jr., in the United States. By organizing nonviolent boycotts, marches, sit-ins, and campaigns of disobedience to legal segregation, King, beginning in 1955, was able to desegregate public facilities in many parts of the American South where segregation had been legally entrenched before. King was helped by white students who continued to use the techniques of civil disobedience outside the South to protest various social and university policies, most strongly the American intervention in Viet Nam. Their sit-ins soon became seizures of buildings.

King himself was felled by an assassin's bullet, as was Gandhi before him. But civil disobedience continues to be used frequently in the U.S., particularly by students, by pacifists, and by black groups. However, it no longer is wholly separated from violence, or limited to specific demands within the system. In Europe civil disobedience is used occasionally as a protest against armaments (England); or, by Daniele Dolci, against economic neglect (Sicily); in Asia and Africa it has been used to support a variety of religious, ethnic, linguistic and national demands.

7. Gandhi's repudiation of pressure (p. 109).

Melville, Lincoln and Jefferson

While many literary and philosophical works stress the duty of the individual to resist unjust laws, others stress his duty to obey. Thus, the Bible depicts Abraham as having so totally surrendered his individual feelings and scruples to God's authority as to be willing to sacrifice his son Isaac at God's command. (God stayed his hand, thereby marking the final rejection of human sacrifice by the Jews.)

In America, where individual rights usually have been regarded as natural since independence was won, Herman Melville, toward the end of his life, affirmed the duty of authority to override individual rights for the sake of *raison d'état* in the novel *Billy Budd*. Impressed, in time of war, from the British merchantman *The Rights of Man* onto H.M.S. *Indomitable,* the sailor Billy Budd (an incarnation of prelapsarian innocence) is falsely accused of mutinous conspiracy. When Captain Vere (the name is not accidental) asks him to defend himself, Budd loses his power of speech and discharges his anger by striking his accuser, the satanic master at arms Claggart, who falls dead. Knowing the circumstances and personalities involved, the immediately convoked court martial thinks that "Budd purposed neither mutiny nor homicide" and is reluctant to convict him. Captain Vere, too, feels Budd to be innocent, yet insists that in "the clash of military duty with moral scruple, . . . private conscience should yield to that imperial one" which requires the death sentence. Else, the sailors, many impressed into service as Budd had been, would feel that a mutinous act had been condoned; they might be en-couraged to mutiny themselves. Budd is convicted; the need for the sentence is explained to him by the captain. As he is hanged he cries: "God bless Captain Vere," and from "the ship's populace . . . came a resonant sympathetic echo—'God bless Captain Vere.'" Authority and order have been preserved by the sacrifice of innocence. The ship of state sails on. Although Billy is more Greek than Hebrew, one may speculate that his author interpreted the Gospels (as Dostoyevsky did before him) and found Pontius Pilatus was in duty bound to forgo justice to the individual in favor of law and order.[8] At any rate Melville clearly displays an ultra-Hobbesian view: the preservation of social order may require the sacrifice of innocents, of individual rights, and of individual conscience, and this sacrifice may be justified in the light of reason.

The justification of the sacrifice of innocence, and the juxtaposition of *raison d'état* and individualism, are historically un-American, but the insistence on obedience is not. Abraham Lincoln in his 1838 address "The Perpetuation of Our Political Institutions" fervidly exhorted his audience:

> Let every American, every lover of liberty, every well wisher to his posterity, swear by the blood of the Revolution, never to violate in the least particular, the laws of the country; and never to tolerate their violation by others . . . Let reverence for the laws . . . be taught in schools, in seminaries and in colleges . . . let it be preached from the pulpit, proclaimed in the legislative halls, and enforced in courts of justice. And, in short, let it become *the political religion* of the nation; . . .
>
> although bad laws, if they exist, should be repealed as soon as possible, still while they continue in force, for the sake of example, they should be religiously observed . . . There is no grievance that is a fit object of redress by mob law.

Thomas Jefferson, who denied the authority of the Supreme Court to overrule the Congress, was consistent, and no less ardent, when, in his First Inaugural Address (1801) he demanded: ". . . absolute acquiescence in the decisions of the

8. Jesus as savior of, and from, law and order (p. 109).

majority . . . from which there is no appeal but to force, the . . . immediate parent of despotism."

The tension between the requirements of social order and those of justice to individuals is necessarily reflected in the tension between the law and the individual conscience. It is inherent in at least those social organizations in which individuals become conscious of their individuality. What are the arguments for civil obedience, or disobedience, for social authority, or individual conscience?

Arguments for Civil Obedience

To recognize the legitimacy of a government is to recognize its authority to make laws; for, to govern is to make laws. Whatever else they may be, laws are rules that must be obeyed. One cannot, then, recognize the government's authority to make laws and claim the right to disobey them, for the claim would deny the authority one has consented to: to grant the authority to make rules *is* to accept the obligation to obey them. Nor can one claim the right to disobey *some* laws. Each law is a law only inasmuch as it excludes the right to disobey. Else, it would be a suggestion, not a law. Hence, obedience to all laws is the duty of all persons who recognize the authority of the government that makes them.

Further, one who claims for himself the right to disobey laws when they are inconsistent with superior obligations to his conscience, must concede this right to others as well (unless he asserts that only his conscience is superior to law). Thus, to grant the right to disobey laws to anybody, is to grant this right to everybody, if his conscience tells him to disobey. Obedience would become voluntary and the law would be shorn of its binding, i.e., its legal character, to be reduced, once more, to a suggestion. However, suggestions are not enough. Laws must obligate and finally compel, because not everybody voluntarily acts as they enjoin; else, laws would be pointless. They are necessary, because conscience guides individuals and groups into conflicts—settled by making and enforcing laws. Laws, then, are meant to obligate dissenters no less than assenters: else, they would be redundant. Legislative authority is needed to enforce in action the unanimity so often lacking in opinion and desire.

Without laws to proscribe some acts (e.g., murder, or theft, or driving on the wrong side of the street) and prescribe others (e.g., the payment of taxes needed to enforce laws) there could be no social order and no viable society. Activities would be disorganized. Naked and arbitrary power would prevail in all conflicts and "the life of man" would be "solitary, poor, nasty, brutish and short" (Hobbes). Yet, as soon as the distribution of power is stabilized, it generates a social order, a set of enforced rules accepted as moral obligations—law. Barely conceivable, a lawless society cannot exist.*

Arguments for Civil Disobedience

The question: when, if ever, and to what extent, is it a *moral* duty to obey the law? is prior to, and independent of the legal question (Do I have a *legal* duty to obey?) and of prudential questions (Can I get away with it? How effective is disobedience as a

---

* *Ubi societas, ibi lex* the Romans said: wherever there is a society, there is law.

means to my ends?) The morality of specific laws too becomes relevant only after the general moral obligation to obey all, none, or only some laws, has been decided. On what grounds, then, can the general moral obligation to obey laws be rejected or qualified?*

Obedience to law is rejected altogether by (1) anarchists (they believe that no government has legitimate authority which need be obeyed); it is qualified by (2) legitimists (they believe that only some governments are legitimate and need be obeyed); finally its extent is limited by (3) those who believe that all governments need be obeyed only as long as they do not violate prior and superior moral principles, such as may be established by religion, nature ("nature" may include the nature of human society, and of human beings), reason and individual conscience. Although justifications for civil disobedience often are combined, it will be convenient to examine them separately.

1. The Anarchist Argument

Anarchists reject the moral duty to obey laws because they regard laws as unnecessary and likely to intensify the very evils—coercion, inefficiency, conflict, oppression, injustice and suffering —they are to reduce. Anarchists feel that people are, or could be, so goodnatured that no laws are needed to restrain them, to settle conflicts, or even to organize activities such as traffic or commerce. Decentralization could reduce the need for rules, and, with sufficient institutional changes, the rules still needed would be spontaneously established and voluntarily followed. Each person would follow the rules he approves because he approves them, and not because he has an obligation to obey. There would

---

* Any qualification presupposes rejection of Thomas Hobbes' view that "the laws are the rules of just and unjust," shared, in sophisticated form, by the late Hans Kelsen.

be no authority, no obligation to anything external to oneself, no compulsion, and no sanctions.

The anarchist view rests, at least in part, on factual assumptions about possible, or probable, human behavior. However, it is usually so formulated that it cannot be proved, or disproved, by any evidence available, or even conceivable. Nonetheless, so far, observation of infants and of primitive societies does not support the anarchist view of the possibilities of human conduct in differently conditioned societies. Nor is the anarchist view supported by experience with communities based on it, or with societies attempting to enact it. Anarchists attribute this to unfavorable conditions, or to wrong methods or, sometimes, to the prior conditioning of the observer and the observed.

Ancient writers (e.g., Ovid in his *Metamorphoses*,* drawing, in turn, on much earlier sources) imagined a golden age of spontaneous harmony such as is also depicted in the biblical paradise.[9] (The Bible indicates but one law—which was violated.) Anarchists rely on faith ("the evidence of things not seen"), as do Christians, although anarchists usually do not acknowledge such reliance. They expect to regain paradise by human action, and, unlike Christians, within history. So do Marxists. Yet the eschatological expectations of either do not seem nearer fulfillment than those of the Christian religion. The latter are not subject to historical proof. But Marxists and anarchists promise fulfillment within history—and the history of their attempts to fulfill their promises is profoundly discouraging.

Marxists (with exceptions) believe in a highly coercive and centralized "dictatorship of the proletariat" in the interim (before the state "withers away") to be established by revolution. Even

---

* *Sponte sua, sine lege fidem rectumque colebat . . . erant sine iudice tuti* (Without law everybody kept promises spontaneously, and acted justly . . . without a judge all were secure).

9. Utopians (p. 110).

democratic Marxists believe in compulsory laws. Most anarchists, however, believe that the coercive state is best abolished by peaceful and noncoercive resistance to its laws, whenever these require "unjust" actions. (Some anarchists, mainly Bakunin and his followers, believe in individual violence, and some in collective violence.) Hence, civil disobedience is approved by anarchists who often attribute the disappointing outcome of revolutions to the coercive methods of revolutionaries. (But one need not be an anarchist to approve of civil disobedience: Socrates was not; nor was Sir Thomas More.)

Some anarchists, notably Max Stirner (1806–1856), and, today, perhaps most coherently R. P. Wolff,* so define each man's obligation to make his own moral choices (autonomy) that it becomes inconsistent with any moral duty to obey the law, i.e., other men (heteronomy). Preferring autonomy, they reject the duty to obey the law. (Their preference may, but need not, involve the theory of spontaneous human harmony mentioned above.)

Political philosophers, such as John Locke and J. J. Rousseau, have tried to show that, at least in a democracy, the moral obligation to obey the law is consistent with the duty—which they acknowledge—to make one's own moral decisions. According to Wolff they succeeded with unanimous, but not with majority decisions—the only ones likely to occur.** The members of the minority, who oppose the majority decision, can accept the (social) responsibility to do what they feel is contrary to their (individual) moral duty only to the extent to which they renounce their moral autonomy. The authority of laws one opposes, one's duty to obey them, can be granted only if one has given up his obligation to keep his entire moral autonomy, if one has

---

* *In Defense of Anarchism* (New York: Harper & Row, 1970)

** The success is trivial of course: a unanimous decision is, by definition, also my own decision.

vested the legislature with a moral authority he has no right to delegate to it, or to anyone.

To refute this anarchist argument, one or more of the elements which makes it seem compelling must be changed: (a) empirical assumptions, (b) definition, or (c) moral preference.

a. By accepting the authority of the law, and thereby giving up, in the short run, some of his actual autonomy, the individual may, in the long run, increase his (potential) autonomy and the autonomy of all other individuals, which, in the absence of law, would be decreased by arbitrary power. If one's obligation is to maximize the effective autonomy of each and all over the long run, it might best be fulfilled by accepting the authority of the law. (The anarchist view of human nature may deny this, but as an empirical matter only.)

b. Anarchists argue that, however justified, a duty to obey commands contrary to one's own felt moral duty, implies giving up one's moral autonomy by recognizing a (heteronomous) authority superior to it. With respect to any particular law they are surely correct. But, if obedience to law, acceptance of social authority, serves the long run maximization of the autonomy of all (freedom) then the short run reduction of each individual's autonomy (legal restriction) may lead to a net gain both in the autonomy of all and in his own. Now, whether this "trade off" is considered an increase, or a renunciation of individual autonomy hinges on whether one defines "individual autonomy" as long run maximization of the moral freedom of all individuals, or as each individual's duty to decide autonomously in each instance. If the first definition is accepted, we have an increase, and if the second is, a loss of "individual autonomy" through acceptance of the duty to obey the law.

c. Finally, one may simply prefer social order—and what is produced by it—to individual autonomy wherever they clash, by regarding the former as a prior moral value, even where it does not enhance the individual autonomy of each person.

2. The Legitimist Argument (Applied to Democracy)

Whereas anarchists regard no government as legitimate, legitimists feel morally bound to obey the laws of legitimate governments, but not of governments they do not regard as legitimate. Although they may follow laws they approve of, or obey as a matter of prudence, legitimists do not feel morally obligated to obey, unless they recognize as legitimate the government which makes, or validates, the laws.

Democrats may not recognize the legitimacy of a nondemocratic government and not feel bound by its laws. Nondemocrats may not feel bound by the laws of a democracy, if they do not regard democratic government as legitimate. Since both governments claim legitimacy, neither can recognize a moral—let alone a legal—right to disobey. To do so would deny its own claim to legitimacy.* All governments claim to be legitimate. But in modern times the claim of democracies is most widely accepted; discussion may be restricted to this claim then.

By definition, in a democracy the citizens decide who shall make laws and thereby consent to be governed by the laws made. Since they elect it and retain the right to oust it, any democratic government has lawmaking authority by consent of at least the majority of citizens. The minority can freely influence the majority, and the legislative process, by persuasion and by voting; it consents to being governed by the prevailing majority, because it retains those (civil) liberties which are required to grow into a majority by persuasion.[10] For these reasons disobedience to law in a democracy, to the extent to which it is successful without persuading the majority, replaces the will of the majority with that of the minority. Civil disobedience which succeeds without

* For a discussion of Dworkin's contrary view see Appendix B (p. 35).
10. Hook on democracy (p. 110).

persuading is called *coercive* civil disobedience. Majority government, legitimate from the democratic viewpoint, is replaced, at least in part, by illegitimate (nondemocratic) minority government which imposes its view on the majority it can not persuade. Despite the moral and libertarian impulse so often behind civil disobedience, the minority government would have to curtail the people's liberties to keep itself in power, or to continue the policies imposed on the unpersuaded majority.[11]

From a strictly democratic viewpoint, then, disobedience to law, ranging from civil disobedience to revolution, is justified only if the citizens have no legitimate ways to freely elect or oust the government by majority vote, i.e., to participate in the lawmaking process—if democracy does not extend to them. Those who are hopelessly and permanently bereft of the right to persuade and vote are under no moral obligation to obey laws imposed on them. This is the situation of all citizens in a nondemocratic system; but some citizens may be in this situation in a democratic one. (In the past economic, sexual, racial and other qualifications for the democratic franchise often were quite restrictive in America. At present they are not; some controversy over these formal qualifications remains, but it is so marginal that it may be neglected; *de facto* qualifications, although fewer than in the past, are still restrictive in a few places. But disenfranchisement has become exceptional.)

Those disenfranchised in a democratic system may try (often with the help of some of the enfranchised) to persuade the government to enfranchise them. As a last resort they may do so by engaging in *persuasive* civil disobedience. Since, usually, a minority is disenfranchised by a majority (or, at any rate, by a more powerful group) persuasion is more likely to be effective than violence, or even nonviolent coercion. The recent past in the U.S. indicates that persuasive civil disobedience can be effective; under the circumstances noted it seems morally legitimate.

11. Local and overall majorities; conflict of majorities (p. 110).

Persuasion, by definition, is always possible in a democracy (though not necessarily successful), and, since democracy aspires to the consent of all citizens, persuasion has usually succeeded in enlarging the franchise. However, in a nondemocratic system attempts at persuasion are likely to be repressed. Since its legitimacy does not rest on continuous consent of the citizens, a nondemocratic government is not likely to be persuaded for the sake of achieving it. Revolution may be the only effective resort for those who oppose the law, or their own disenfranchisement.

Marxists (except for democratic Marxists) and other revolutionary groups harder to classify, may reject the moral obligation to obey the law in a democracy by insisting that constitutional and representative democracy is not "truly" democratic, and can become so only if some groups (reactionaries, capitalists) are altogether disenfranchised, and the economy is socialized.* To them only a Marxist democracy—which bears a suspicious resemblance to a dictatorship of Marxists, euphemistically described as "dictatorship of the proletariat"—is legitimate. They feel morally obligated only by the laws of their own revolutionary government, which is said to derive its authority from the consent of "history," though not necessarily of historians, or of the governed. Since these groups are not interested in changing particular laws as much as in assuming power, they are more likely to prepare for revolution than for civil disobedience.[12]

3. The Argument for Limitation of All Legitimate Authority

Much as they accept the duty to obey the laws of a legitimate government, few legitimists will regard this duty as unbounded. To do so would mean to surrender all individual moral judgment,

---

* See pp. 78ff. for discussion of "true" vs. "formal" democracy.
12. Arrow's problem and democracy (p. 112).

all autonomy, to social authority. However legitimate they may think it, however much they may consent to it in principle, and regard it as necessary, and preferable to any alternative, few will be willing, or able, to surrender their own moral judgment altogether without reservation, to even the best government.

Suppose we regard a democratic government as legitimate; a *prima facie* obligation to obey its laws follows. But suppose, now, an outrageous law is enacted, e.g., a law commanding that all members of a group—redheads, Albigensians, or Jews—be wantonly killed. (Note "wantonly"—matters might differ, if a plausible case for the necessity of killing them could be made.) Democratic freedoms and safeguards, though unimpaired, prove unavailing: the majority can not be persuaded to change the law. The government supporting the law is reelected in a free election and the courts declare the outrageous law constitutional. It is hard to believe that one is morally bound to obey it—that the legitimacy of (democratic) procedure, of majority decision, of courts, or of any authority, generates a moral obligation to obey so immoral a law, or absolves anyone from the moral duty to resist it by illegal, and, perhaps, violent means when legal means are unavailing.

To say as much is to say that the individual conscience can be morally right and legitimate authority wrong; and that in some cases the individual should act illegally to make his conscience prevail over legitimate authority. If authority always, or never, were wrong, we would have the duty to disobey it always, or never. And so with conscience. But if authority is only sometimes wrong, and our conscience only sometimes right, we need a rule to determine when either is—when to obey our conscience and when to obey the law, for we have obligations to both, and they may be in conflict.

The Perennial Conflict

St. Paul declared governments to be "ordained by God" so that "whosoever resisteth them, resisteth the ordinance of God" (Romans 13:1–10); but the apostle Peter thought that "we ought to obey God rather than men" (Acts 5:29). The potential conflict between the duty to obey authority and the duty to obey "God" has never been, and can not be, fully resolved—until in the life to come these obligations become identical.

Conflict can be eluded, or defined away, only by discarding one of the two conflicting moral obligations: the moral duty to follow one's conscience, even if disobeying authority, at least in some cases; or, the moral duty to obey authority, even if disobeying one's conscience, in most but not in all cases.

Thomas Hobbes eliminated the potential conflict between authority and conscience by arguing, with St. Paul, that the duty to obey authority is *always* superior to (or identical with) any other. Anarchists avoid the conflict between conscience and the obligation to obey legitimate authority by asserting that there is no legitimate authority, and, therefore, never a moral duty to obey it. But those who believe that there is (ordinarily) a moral duty to obey legitimate authority, but also (extraordinarily) a moral duty to disobey it (when it promulgates morally monstrous laws) face a problem: how do we know when to obey and when to disobey? *when* to listen to our conscience and *when* to the law? By what *general* rule can we decide and justify our decision?

The Individual Conscience

The voice of his individual conscience may suffice for the conscientious objector, who claims no more than that the legal duty, the command of authority, is conscientiously (and perhaps idiosyncratically) so repugnant to him that he can not carry it out. Even if he asserts more—that to obey this law is morally wrong for everybody—he does not profess that it is his responsibility to make everybody disobey the law. But to engage in civil disobedience, let alone violent resistance, is to claim no less. It is to demand that everybody (not just those who feel they should) must disobey, that nobody has an obligation, or even a right, to obey the law of the legitimate government which legally commands us to do a morally monstrous thing. Thus, the consciences of the legitimate authority and, in a democracy, of its majority supporters, and the obligation to obey the law, are subordinated to the dictates of the conscience of the minority which engages in civil disobedience. But our conscience can supersede that of others only if, unlike some traditional conscientious objectors, we claim to voice moral rules binding on all, and capable of invalidating those proclaimed by others. Whence these superior moral principles?

Some Unsuccessful Answers

Attempts to indicate when the duty of disobedience replaces the duty of obedience to legitimate authority usually rely on norms, or principles, thought to be superior to the positive law of governments because they emanate from nature or God—from an authority superior to that of human legislators. Recognized by reason, these norms are thought to invalidate any positive law which violates them.

A government may accept these superior principles and contend that its positive law conforms to them. If citizens disagree, the government may subordinate itself to a decision, for instance, by ecclesiastical authority, and avoid conflict at the price of sovereignty (independence from any superior authority). But if the jurisdiction of a superior authority is rejected by the government or by the opposition—whether or not either professes belief in the superior norms to be applied by that authority—conflicts about the validity of a positive law, produced by different interpretations of the superior natural or divine norms, cannot be resolved. The faithful citizen will have to decide for himself which side to take. And he will be wrong in the eyes of at least one of the parties, as St. Thomas More was.

Fallible Interpretations

If it be assumed that the accepted (e.g., ecclesiastical) authority is infallible, the moral duty of all faithful citizens and rulers is to obey its interpretations of superior law, and to relinquish their own. They must disobey any contrary inferior authority, be it their legitimate government or their conscience. However, if the accepted authority is not thought to be infallible by either party, if it can be wrong, then its interpretation can not *ultimately* settle disagreements on natural, or divine, law. Its decision may be rejected by either those who support, or by those who oppose, the validity of a positive law in the light of their interpretation of natural or divine norms.

Any fallible authority could misinterpret norms; it may even support a morally monstrous positive law. History offers all too many illustrations. Thus, both temporal and ecclesiastical authorities supported the Holy Office of the Inquisition. At best the fallible authority would be in the position of the U.S. Supreme Court, which interprets the Constitution to determine the validity of laws legislated by other authorities: its interpretation of the Constitution may not satisfy those who do not share it; and it could conceivably be, or become, morally monstrous.* The citizen convinced that this has occurred would have to follow his conscience instead. But his conscience, unfortunately, is not infallible either.

Nature, scripture, principles, laws, or constitutions, however high their source, or authority, require interpretation; they always can be interpreted to support what our conscience may call on us to disobey as monstrously immoral. Unless they postulate an infallible interpretative authority, such as never has been universally accepted in history, theories which set out to resolve the conflict between the moral duty to obey legitimate authority, and the moral duty to disobey it sometimes, evade the problem when they appeal to the higher authority of reason, nature, or God. For the problem is not *whether* positive laws should be disobeyed when contrary to natural law, divine law or to any other authority; the problem is how to decide *when* they are.

And the principles which might decide this require interpretation. To entrust that interpretation to any fallible authority is to embark on an infinite regress; for that authority can be wrong—and so can any fallible authority superior to it. To entrust this interpretation to the individual conscience is no better since it, too, is fallible. Further, to leave the decision to the individual conscience is to give up any rule morally binding on all, including differing consciences.[13] Thus, unless an infallible interpretative authority is assumed, there can be no ultimate operative standard

* The power of the Supreme Court to enforce its decisions is, of course, irrelevant to any moral obligation to follow it.

13. "Moral rule" defined as inconsistent with rule of individual conscience (p. 114).

to determine *when* to disobey legitimate authority. Merely to point to superior standards is to confuse the question with the answer.[14]

The tension between individual conscience and social authority is an aspect of the tension between the individual and the group. It can be obscured by defining "law" and "morality" so that they must coincide, or become irrelevant to each other. But to eliminate contradictions in description is not to eliminate conflicts in the experience described, in behavior, and in emotion. These conflicts can not be resolved (although, of course, on each occasion they are settled one way or another) because the moral realm resists full absorption, or exhaustion, by the legal realm, the individual by the social. We must live with these conflicts.[15]

Civil Disobedience as a Social Problem

Lack of theoretical solution in no way relieves us of the practical need to find the best solution possible; we must try to minimize conflicts in number and extent, so as to reduce injury to individuals and to the social fabric.[16]

Now, if one rejects (1) Hobbes's proposal to eliminate the problem by discarding the individual conscience and any notion of justice beyond the law and (2) the anarchist proposal to eliminate the problem by discarding legitimate social authority; if, further, (3) one does not think that infallible moral authority

14. "Natural law" explored (p. 115).
15. No evidence for solubility of conflicts (p. 117).
16. Useful conflicts? (p. 117).

is available in this world and (4) acknowledges that all fallible authorities (whatever the rules in which their decisions rest) are, by definition, vulnerable to the point of irrelevance, since their decision never can be final in the moral sense; if finally, (5) one acknowledges that conscience is fallible as well and, anyway, (6) capable of creating a morally binding social rule only for those who agree on its pronouncements—which certainly describes the problem and not the solution; if, then, one gives assent to these six conclusions, how is the recurrent problem to be dealt with?

The following partly moral, partly prudential, standards suggest when moral disagreement warrants civil disobedience, and when it does not. They are, of course, no less open to differing interpretation (without a conclusive interpretative authority) than the moral standards which give rise to the disagreement in the first place. Nonetheless they are worth listing; for they seem rational, and, if widely accepted, they may reduce the frequency of unproductive or counterproductive civil obedience.

One is morally justified to deliberately disobey legitimate authority if (a) the protested law is morally intolerable to him and (b) not likely to be remedied otherwise; and (c) the effects of the law are not revokable by probable or possible later correction; and if (d) the totality of the expected effects of civil disobedience under the circumstance is, in his view, morally preferable to the totality of expected effects of any of the courses available within the law.[17]

The last two points might benefit from illustration. The U.S. Supreme Court found that President Roosevelt did not violate the Constitution when, during World War II, he confined vast numbers of U.S. citizens of Japanese ancestry to camps away from their homes, thus depriving them of livelihood, property, and home, without hearings, or any showing of military necessity or individual guilt. Some people felt then, and many agree now, that the action was morally and constitutionally wrong, un-

17. "Totality of effects" interpreted (p. 117).

needed, and outrageous. Yet, if not reversible (few actions are) the measure was revokable. Indeed, although they certainly suffered hardships (as so many guiltless citizens and soldiers did during the war) these people were able, in time, once more to enjoy the full benefits of their citizenship. Dissent certainly was justifiable in this occasion, but not civil disobedience. For the damage done was revokable. (Executions would not have been). And civil disobedience in wartime might have been ineffective and, if effective, calamitous: the totality of its effects probably would have been morally worse than the effect of not engaging in it.

Coercive Civil Disobedience

The standards for coercive civil disobedience in a democracy can be particularized then. If one believes in the legitimacy of the government, yet is outraged by a law or policy which, despite persuasion, despite even persuasive civil disobedience, the majority continues to support, coercive civil disobedience—and ultimately, insurrection—is justifiable if (1) the effects of the law (or policy) at issue are irrevokable and outrageous enough to prefer giving up democratic government to living with that law or policy; (2) there is reason to believe that coercion of the majority which supports the outrageous law or policy may be effective (this is unlikely but not impossible); (3) the ensuing minority policy and dictatorship, independent of, and imposed on the majority (and which necessarily restricts its freedom) seems, *in toto*, morally preferable to the outrages of the majority government. It is well to remember here Sidney Hook's dictum "The democrat . . . knows that the majority can be wrong; but he will not . . . accept the rule of a minority because it occasionally may be right; . . . the process by which a minority may . . . become . . . a majority is all important . . ."*

* "The Ideology of Violence," *Encounter* (April, 1970).

Our assumption here has been that the majority remains un-persuaded and has to be coerced, its government overthrown to replace the law or policy at issue. Without this assumption there would be no case for coercive civil disobedience, unless the coercion is applied to a local authority, or on a limited issue, in the hope of producing the support of the overall majority. Such limited coercive civil disobedience requires an outrage more severe than persuasive civil disobedience does, but not as severe as to lead one to prefer dictatorship to democratic majority government.

The outrages which would justify coercive civil disobedience in a democracy fortunately are rare. (However, settlers—though not quite democratically governed—have come near hunting down native populations. And the foreign and domestic policies of democracies all too often have violated the standards pro-fessed by their citizens.) No democracy has ever attempted to imprison, and then to exterminate, defenseless political, social, or racial groups of citizens or foreigners. Dictatorships have done so all too frequently. Wherefore it seems unlikely that replace-ment of a democratic majority regime doing "bad" things, with a nondemocratic minority regime not doing them (at first), is likely to improve matters effectively in the long run. Yet this is the only alternative to persuasion. Thus, the effectiveness at least of coercive civil disobedience in attaining its ultimate, as dis-tinguished from its temporary aim, must be doubted, in most cases.

Persuasive Civil Disobedience

Persuasive civil disobedience is justifiable (and preferable to coercive civil disobedience) whenever the laws and practices protested outrage one's moral feeling sufficiently to be intolerable but the effects are revokable, and one still hopes to persuade the majority; or, if one does not feel the issue warrants overthrowing democratic government in favor of a minority dictatorship which may make matters worse in the end. Neither coercive nor persuasive civil disobedience can be justified if the issue is of less than overwhelming moral importance, or if persuasion by legal means is possible and not altogether hopeless.

APPENDIX A:

Some Marginal Arguments

Social Change

1. Persuasive civil disobedience is sometimes urged in a democracy as necessary to bring about "social change." Empirically one may doubt that civil disobedience is a necessary or effective means to do so. (Immense social changes have occurred in the U.S. and England without civil disobedience.) If it were necessary, civil disobedience would not be justified thereby, unless the desirability of the change achieved through it and the desirability of achieving it by these means, also were shown. Such a showing could not add to the arguments in favor of persuasive civil disobedience which have been discussed already.[18]

Acceptance of Punishment

2. Occasionally it is argued that the willingness of those guilty of civil disobedience to "accept" their punishment exculpates them morally. Such willingness attests to their sincerity and seriousness. But it adds nothing else to the merit of their actions.

18. Does efficiency justify "direct action"? (p. 118).

No offense—be it a parking violation, a theft, or public-spirited civil disobedience—can be justified by "accepting" punishment for it. The punishment declares the wrongness of the act punished; "acceptance" indicates the recognition thereof by the offender. Acceptance can not justify what it recognizes to be wrong.

The moral obligation to obey the law can never be satisfied by submitting to the punishment for not obeying it. Such submission merely satisfies the (different) obligation to submit. Else, "acceptance" of a punishment would have to be regarded as a moral license to commit crimes or as a *post facto* assertion of a "right" to do so. One would have to hold a rather odd exchange theory of criminal law to conclude that an offender, by "accepting" punishment buys a retroactive license to offend. On the contrary, the punishment is to deter, not to license, regardless of whether burglars are involved, or people engaged in civil disobedience.

In addition to being fallacious, the view that acceptance of punishment justifies civil disobedience also seems irrelevant. The acceptance of punishment by those engaged in civil disobedience has been correctly interpreted, since Socrates' days, as a sign not of repentance, but of insistence on the moral wrongness of the law the offender protests against by his disobedience. Since it signifies continued defiance, rather than a promise to henceforth obey the law, acceptance of punishment in civil disobedience cases does not reduce the need for punishment and cannot serve as an extenuating circumstance—unlike the moral motivation of the offender which might be so considered.*

---

* Of course, these considerations do not apply when the offender actually repents his offense and promises lawful conduct in the future.

Nuremberg

3. Legal precedents, such as the Nuremberg trials, occasionally have been used as justifications for civil disobedience.* To the extent to which the Nuremberg precedent concerns offenses against "the laws and customs of war" it does not add to domestic legislation to which one may appeal more easily. Where the precedent went beyond domestic legislation, e.g., by branding the waging of "aggressive war" as a crime, it was not regarded as applicable, in Nuremberg, or anywhere else, to volunteer or drafted soldiers, or to officers of any rank. The precedent was applied exclusively against political leaders thought to have conspired to bring about the "aggressive war" (in practice one might replace "aggressive" with "lost," certainly a necessary, if not a sufficient characteristic of the legal ascription of "aggressive"). This precedent, therefore, cannot justify resisting the draft, or refusing to fight, though it might justify an indictment of political leaders.[19]

* If these precedents are valid, rather than disobeying the law, the protester will be asserting his legal rights (and obligations) against the unlawful orders of an authority.

19. Nuremberg trials as precedents (p. 118).

APPENDIX B:

Dworkin on Laws and Moral Rights

Ronald Dworkin, Professor of Jurisprudence at Oxford, has tried to redefine the relation between what he calls "moral rights" (which do not seem to differ significantly from "natural rights," except that their provenience is even more obscure) and legal rights.* Because the ideas proffered are widely, if vaguely, shared and are argued by Professor Dworkin with as much sophistication as I have seen, I have added the scrutiny hereinafter following.

Dworkin argues that one has "a moral right to break any law that the government, by virtue of his right, had no right to adopt"; and "Any society that claims to recognize rights at all must abandon the notion of a general duty to obey the law . . . if a citizen argues that he has a moral right . . . to protest in a way he finds effective . . . then an official . . . can not point . . . to a Supreme Court decision as having . . . decisive weight"; finally, "Anyone who thinks that the government view [on what is lawful] is necessarily the correct view must believe that men and women have only such moral rights as government chooses to grant, which means that they have no moral rights at

* See *New York Review of Books,* June 6, 1968 and December 17, 1970.

all." Here (and throughout) it is suggested that individuals have "moral rights" which exist independently of any rights granted by the government.

Claims and Rights

It is a truism that individuals wish the government to recognize moral claims (which, indeed, are formed independently) so that they may become legal rights through this recognition. Dworkin, however, argues that, if an individual asserts a moral claim, the assertion makes his claim a moral *right;* and that this asserted "moral right" should be recognized *ipso facto* as a *legal* right. What I call a claim, then, is to Dworkin a "moral right"; and he urges that no contrary legal prohibition ought to be enforced against the claimant. He should not be punished for violating a law which prohibits what he asserts he has a "moral right" to do or for violating a law which commands what he asserts he has a "moral right" not to do. Thus the "moral right" must be treated as a superseding legal right.

Now, people certainly have moral claims. But they have only such (legal) rights as are granted by the government. The idea of "moral rights" which are not rights granted by law, but yet have legal force, or, as we have seen, force superior to law, and are, therefore, more than (moral) claims, strikes me as very odd (despite the long history of "natural rights"*). Rights are granted by a rights-granting authority. If any body has that status and I accept its legitimacy, I have only the rights granted by it. Beyond these, I retain only claims; I can not have rights "against" that body. Rights are by definition social: they always involve restrictions on, or duties of, others. A right is a permission to do, or obtain something, or a promise—always by, or from society; or else a right is protection against suffering something

* See pp. 25–27 and Fn. 14 (p. 115).

in, or being deprived of something by, society. Who but society (others) could permit, promise, protect? And in any society who could grant or validate rights other than the government?[20]

Moral Claims, Natural Rights?

Dworkin's belief that moral claims may be morally more justifiable than contrary law is neither novel nor problematic. However, the legal force attributed to the claims he calls "moral rights" is. He thinks that the courts should not enforce a positive law whenever a "moral right" is in conflict with it (there is no issue otherwise). Wherein is this more than a decently obscure, but otherwise unsupported and puzzling return to natural law and natural rights theories, leaving unsolved all the problems that led Bentham, John Stuart Mill and Austin—let alone later jurisprudence—to discard these theories? A natural rights theory to guide legislation is intelligible and consistent with the administration of positive law. But Dworkin's theory would *replace* positive law and adjudication with the assertion of moral rights. Did they accept Dworkin's view, the courts would have to consider a set of asserted "moral rights" in addition to the positive law (which in the U.S. includes the Constitution), and when the asserted "moral rights" are in conflict with the positive law, they would have to set it aside. The assertion of "moral rights" would thus become an act of legislation superseding all constitutional or congressional legislation and all precedents. To be sure, in each case the courts would have to ratify the "moral rights." But only in a prudential sense, for the "moral rights" to be ratified would be independent of the courts. And ratification would necessarily become as unpredictable as the "moral rights" themselves. The courts could not be guided, let alone bound, by legislation in accepting or rejecting "moral rights," otherwise,

20. Anarchism and obligation (p. 119).

moral right would depend on legislation after all. Individuals, in short, could assert moral rights despite or beyond legislation.

Dworkin's further view, that one who does not believe in moral rights "thinks that the government view is necessarily the correct view" does not follow from his own belief in "moral rights" or from anything else. The view that individuals have no rights beyond those "government chooses to grant" does not imply the belief that "the government view is necessarily the correct view"; nor is the former implied by the latter belief. The only implication is that the government alone has rights-granting authority. Nothing whatever is suggested, let alone entailed, about the correctness of the government's exercise thereof. Consent to such authority need not be based on any belief about correctness of exercise in particular cases.* I may think the government and the court morally, and even legally, wrong in the substantive decision of a case, without questioning its legal authority to make the wrong decision or asserting any legal authority (moral right) to disobey. Essentially this was Socrates' position elaborated in *Crito*.**

Legal and Moral Rights

If the government is incorrect, in my opinion, in granting or withholding legal rights, my view that the government is wrong and should have granted me a right it did not grant me, does not itself grant me that right, or give me a "moral right" to disobey laws, and to act as though I had the legal right which the government refused to grant me. I might, indeed, wish to over-

---

* See also the anarchist argument pp. 15–18. Readers may be reminded of the Donatist heresy in which Professor Dworkin appears on the Donatist side: he maintains that authority rather than being vested in the office, depends on the virtues of the officeholder and the rightness of his decisions.

** See p. 6.

throw, or, in some cases, to disobey, a government which uses its authority in ways I altogether disapprove; and I might feel morally entitled to overthrow a government which does not rest its authority on my general consent, and gives me no opportunity to oust it by legitimate processes. I may refuse my consent to the authority of such a government (or to any government) and, if I believe that its authority could derive only from the consent I have refused, I may thereupon defy it. But I certainly could not assert a legal right to defiance. Such a legal right would, in effect, ask the authority I wish to defy to grant me the right to defy it, or, at least, to recognize my (inherent?) right to do so (to defy does not mean to oppose or dissent, but to *disobey* legal orders). To urge a legal right to defy valid laws amounts to urging the courts to recognize a legal right (which is asserted to exist independently) to illegally defy them without being legally punished; or else to urge the courts to avoid defiance by not enforcing a valid positive law whenever a "moral right" against it is asserted.

Dworkin's argument, then, appears to rest on a double confusion: (1) of moral claims and legal rights; (2) of the legal (and moral) authority of institutions, and of the correctness of their actions—in the light of legal and moral criteria—in particular instances. It is this confusion which leads him to think that people who engage in civil disobedience have "a right to follow their consciences." There is no issue about their moral claim. There is about the legal status of it. They neither have, nor do they usually assert such a *legal* right. On the contrary, in following their consciences, people usually assert a moral need, or desire, which they recognize to be inconsistent with their legal rights. Their action may at times be defended by *ultra posse nemo obligatur,** but, although inability is a defense for not acting in accordance with the law, it does not grant a right to do

* Nobody can be obligated beyond his ability (to carry out his obligation).

so—any more than inability to support my children relieves me of the obligation to do so when I can.

Dworkin's question: "If a man has a right to do what his conscience tells him he must, then . . . is it not wicked for the state to punish what it acknowledges that men have a right to do?" is answered easily now: it would be wicked if men did have that "right," and if the government were to acknowledge it. They don't and the government doesn't. Hence it is not wicked for the government to punish what it does not acknowledge anyone has a right to do—even though some claim a moral obligation to do it—and, indeed, has legislated to be wrong.

Having asked a misleading question, Dworkin gives an irrelevant answer. He distinguishes between "being right"—i.e., morally entitled—and "having a right"—i.e., being legally free to do something—and concludes that civil disobedience is justifiable because the first somehow leads to the second, or, at least should dissuade from prosecutions when a positive law is violated. This begs the question, i.e., the possible conflict between moral claims or feelings (being right) and legal rights (having rights). The latter is necessarily decided by governmental authority, not by the claimant. Hence the possibility of conflict which Dworkin defines away by instructing authority to recognize all asserted "moral rights."

Prisoners of War

Dworkin's illustration—the right, or duty of a prisoner of war to escape, recognized (but not granted) by the detaining power —does not help him. It illustrates the fact that the prisoner has a superior obligation to the law of his government and none to the contrary law of the detaining power. However, citizens have an obligation to the law of their own government, which in the government's eyes cannot be superseded by any other. No government can see itself in the position of the detaining power with respect to its own citizens; nor can it accept being so regarded.

Anyway, the recognition by the detaining power of the prisoner's nonobligation to it is largely a matter of reciprocity, or generosity. It is prudential in nature: each detaining power recognizes the prisoner's obligation to his own legal system, which imposes the duty to escape, and the implied nonobligation to contrary duties imposed by the legal system of the detaining power. Such recognition rests on the mutual expectation of warring powers that each will act likewise with respect to its captives. Else the prisoner would not be thought "to be right" or "to have a right" to try to escape.

However, a defendant's assertion of nonobligation to the law of his place of residence, his allegation of allegiance to the legal system of a different, higher sovereign (God, conscience, nature, history), could not help him. His allegiance to his conception of law ("moral right") cannot grant him impunity, for such a grant would deny the universal obligatoriness of law—its legal character. I know of no case where such an allegiance has been recognized:* such recognition would entail renunciation of the government's authority to make binding laws. The government's assertion that in making laws it is guided by God, nature, and so on is a different matter. Such an assertion in no sense acknowledges any "moral right" of citizens to defy the positive laws of the government by alleging to be *independently* guided by such sovereigns.

Rights and Constitutions

The issue is unnecessarily confused when Dworkin speaks of certain constitutional rights "against the government" to suggest that rights do not come from, or depend on, the government.

---

* See pp. 4–6 on conscientious objection.

Constitutional rights are rights granted and upheld by (not "against") the constitutional government; else they are neither constitutional nor rights. The *façon de parler* "against the government" actually means against a government official (or office) legislative or executive, alleged to have exceeded or misused his legal authority or to have been remiss in his legal duty. Whereupon the judiciary, another part of the government, is asked to order the official to act in accordance with, but not beyond his lawful authority and, if necessary, to punish him. Thus, rights "against the government" are legal rights only inasmuch as upheld, or granted by the government against one of its officials.

Dworkin's contention that one has "a moral right to break any law that the government, by virtue of his right, had no right to adopt" means one of two things: (1) that one has a legal right to "break" a putative law because the government—i.e., a lower court, or the Congress, or an administrative agency—did not have the legal right to adopt this "law"; the law is invalid (illegal) and the court does, or will, or should find that the citizen acted lawfully by "breaking" the (invalid) law. This is an accepted part of our constitutional process and hardly an issue.* But Dworkin argues (2) that the citizen has "a moral right to break any law" even if and after the courts hold the law to be valid (constitutional). This means that the citizen has a right to overrule the courts, and Dworkin seems to acknowledge as much: "Any society that claims to recognize rights at all must abandon the notion of a general duty to obey the law . . . if a citizen argues that he has a moral right . . . to protest in a way he finds effective[21] . . . then an official . . . can not point . . . to a Supreme Court decision as having . . . decisive weight."

---

* See Fn. 3 (p. 107) on actual and putative laws.
21. Effectiveness and legitimacy (p. 119).

Moralists or Lawyers Propose, Courts Dispose

Now, morally the law and the courts may be wrong, and, in the citizen's view, perhaps legally too. But the courts decide legal matters. Citizens cannot overrule the decision of the courts, or disobey with impunity, unless the courts are to be shorn of this authority. It is the very nature of law to be an obligation superior to the moral views, legal interpretations, and consciences of the individual citizen, who, therefore, cannot have a right (moral, or, above all, legal) to overrule the law as interpreted by the courts, however wrong he thinks the courts are. While no court can morally invalidate a moral claim—the claimant may continue to hold it—courts exist to establish the legal status of moral claims. They alone can do so. They alone can grant or withhold legal rights, whatever the moral claims made. In any legal system moral claims become legal rights only when granted by the government (legislatively or by judicial determination). Whence the Supreme Court must decide whether there is a legal right; and officials have the duty to give "decisive weight" to the Supreme Court's decision, and not to the claimant's or to their own moral views or to asserted "moral rights."

Dworkin goes on to argue that an individual should follow "his own judgment of the law in spite of his judgment that the courts will probably find against him [and] regardless of whether [there is] a contrary decision already on the books" since he is "within his social rights in refusing to accept that decision as conclusive." In one sense this argument is inconsistent with what goes before or, at least, redundant. Why should the citizen bother to form any "judgment of the law" when he can always supersede the law by his "moral rights" or his "social rights"—regardless of what the courts decide? Is this more than a promise to be bound by a court decision—provided it goes your way?

To be sure, nothing ongoing ever is final; and nothing need

be so "accepted." Yet, a citizen must abide by the court's present decision whether it is acceptable to him or not, and regardless of whether he thinks that future courts or laws will be on his side. If Dworkin's reasoning were accepted, the opinions of the courts would be advisory, and could not even be temporarily decisive. Certainly one may continue indefinitely to oppose a court decision on moral, or legal, grounds; but such opposition does not confer a legal right or even a moral right to disobey; nor can one object in principle to enforcement of court decisions contrary to defendants' claims, as Dworkin does, unless one is willing to replace courts and laws by individual consciences. Why enact laws if they are not to be enforced? "Don't enforce," Dworkin urges, "after all, the disobeyed law may be found invalid in the future." But, unless the courts hold the law invalid, or at least questionable, it must be enforced against those who assert it is, when the courts do not. Else, the mere assertion of invalidity would invalidate the law or, at least, would make it unenforceable against those who assert it to be invalid. (Incidentally, people do not usually engage in civil disobedience because they think the law invalid; they think it should be defied despite its legal validity.)

Punishment

With respect to punishment of civil disobedience Dworkin advises defendants to escape: "if a man believes he has a right [not recognized by law] then he is silly . . . to obey the law [or] to accept the punishment the state has no right to give." It is not clear whether Dworkin's "no right to give" means "no authority to give" or "made a wrong use of its authority in giving." If the last interpretation were correct, Dworkin would be saying that anyone who submits to a court decision against him "is silly."

Even if one believes courts have no authority ever to determine the legal status of moral rights, if citizens always have a moral right to defy them, one cannot reject the quite separate moral obligation to submit to punishment. To do so one must separately deny the authority of the courts to inflict it. I may feel a moral obligation to kill X and reject the court's contrary views. But I may still have an obligation to submit to the court's punishment. The rejected moral obligation not to kill X is quite separate from the moral obligation to submit to punishments inflicted by the courts—even if they are punishments meted out for breaking an unjust law. I may even be innocent of the crime the court found me guilty of. Does that mean I have no moral, let alone legal, obligation to submit to its verdict?

At any rate, Dworkin's advice rests on "if a man believes he has a right" and therefore begs the question. The advice implies that the decision as to whether he has a right is up to the man who claims the right—whereas only claiming it is up to him. He has a duty to submit to judicial decision, even when he believes it erroneous. Else all obligation to submit to a legal system to decide conflicts is denied.*

Dworkin also advises authorities to let civil disobedience go unpunished "out of respect for the moral position of its authors" unless it can be shown that civil disobedience will (not may) lead to lawbreaking in general. Why not, then, "out of respect" for the burglar's hunger, or the robber's compulsive envy, let his crime go unpunished if it cannot be shown that this will increase crime in general? "Respect" of motivation together with other considerations may influence the degree of punishment, but not the punishability of the act. The law does not punish, or exempt, because of motivation. (*Mens rea* is enough); effects, too, may influence only the degree of punishment. (I do not believe, incidentally, that impunity can ever be *shown* to lead to lawbreaking. Yet *de facto* impunity probably is one of the major causes of crime rate rises.) Dworkin finally urges "if the number would not increase then the state should leave the dis-

* See Fn. 4 (p. 108).

senters [Dworkin means resisters—not an insignificant *lapsus*] alone," but if the number increases presecution should be given up as well, since obviously people are increasingly against the law. Prosecution, thus, is either unnecessary or inadvisable.

When to Enforce

Dworkin does not indicate when a resisted law should be enforced against resisters. But he argues that citizens, or majorities, have no right to insist on enforcement, e.g., of the draft law, unless they can show how nonenforcement would injure them. Unless resisters can be shown not just to have disobeyed the law, but to have injured U.S. interests thereby, they should not be punished. Contrary to congressional intent, this would make military service voluntary rather than compulsory. Only those citizens would allow themselves to be drafted who think our military activity, and their contribution to it, to be necessary in the national interest. Since a showing of specific injury from nonenforcement would be required before any law could be enforced, the judiciary would have to decide on the wisdom of policies, foreign and domestic. Congress no longer would be able to make enforceable laws within the Constitution: if a law, to be enforceable, would have to be shown to be necessary, the courts, rather than Congress, would decide whether the draft law is really needed to pursue foreign policy, and whether any policy pursued is really needed for American interests, or, perhaps, injurious to them.

Segregationists

Dworkin's argument may be used by a conscientious segregationist against enforcement of desegregation. To counter this, Dworkin maintains that segregation would inflict personal injury on the segregated Negro children who, therefore, could demand enforcement of desegregation laws. Dworkin here ignores his previous views on the nondecisive weight to be given court decisions; for the *Brown* decision—which itself was not supported by the weight of scientific evidence then and now—is the decisive basis for asserting that segregation *per se* is injurious to Negro children. At any rate a segregationist might conscientiously maintain that desegregation inflicts personal injury on the desegregated white children. If that claim is sustained by the courts, desegregation would have no more claim to enforcement than segregation. Dworkin's argument would have deprived both Congress and the Supreme Court of authority to decide the issue, which would be decided, if at all, on the factual findings of harm by the lower courts. Desegregation laws could not be enforced. They can be enforced only if one accepts desegregation as a legal requirement flowing from court decisions which must be followed, even if one regards them as morally, factually or legally doubtful or wrong.* If one does not give decisive weight to court judgments as such, segregationists have no less "right" to disobey the court, than do desegregationists, at least with respect to the legal basis of enforcement.

Blackstone's Silly Saw

Dworkin finally paraphrases Blackstone's silly saw to argue against punishing civil disobedience: "It is better that ten guilty persons escape than that one innocent suffer." Interpreted as a procedural caution, Blackstone's remark means simply that suspects should go free unless the evidence for their guilt is clear. However, the remark is indefensible if interpreted to mean

* I think they are wrong but should be followed because they are validly made decisions.

(using Blackstone's figures): better that ten guilty men—men known to be guilty—should be allowed to go free than that one innocent man—a man known to be innocent—be punished. Since Dworkin argues that those engaged in civil disobedience, even if guilty, should not be punished, he interprets Blackstone in the substantive sense.

Assume Blackstone's proportions—ten guilty men to one innocent man—and assume that the ten men were guilty of assaults that injured their victims. Unpunished and unrehabilitated, they will commit assaults with greater frequency than do people who never were guilty of assault. (Statistics bear out no less.) Therefore, more assaults will be committed than would have been committed had the ten been in prison. Assume now, for simplicity, that the ten guilty men were each spared six months in prison for the sake of the innocent man, and that their future victims are immobilized each for six months by his injuries. Why should the suffering of the several innocent victims of these assaults, which would not have occurred had the guilty men been detained, count for less than the suffering of the one innocent who was spared prison—at the price of the ten guilty men being free to injure these victims? If one assumes further that the punishment of the guilty men would have deterred some assaults by third persons—and all penal systems are based on this assumption—then the failure to punish the ten guilty men further increases the number of innocent people victimized for the sake of not victimizing one innocent man. In short, the maxim proposes something self-defeating: to spare suffering to one innocent, let more than one innocent suffer. The total suffering certainly would exceed what the innocent man was spared.

If legal punishments are ever to be inflicted at all, they sometimes unwittingly will be inflicted on the innocent, such being human frailty. We certainly must make every effort to avoid such injustices; we should by and large follow Blackstone's procedural caution although not to the length of taking his hyperbole literally. A procedure that actually fails to convict ten probably guilty suspects for the sake of not convicting one probably innocent suspect should certainly be changed so as to convict a higher proportion of the guilty. But if we were to follow Blackstone's advice in the substantive interpretation, if we were to let ten men known to be guilty go free for the sake of an innocent man, we would be defeating our purpose altogether. Instead of protecting the innocent and punishing the guilty, we would protect the guilty as well as the innocent and more of the former. By not punishing the guilty we would, in the end, injure more innocents than would have been injured if the courts had not spared the guilty for the sake of the innocents.

Political Violence

Definitions, Distinctions
and Continuities

Ways of Obtaining Compliance

In all societies numerous ways of obtaining compliance coexist. Violence is one way. To locate it politically, one must specify the relation of violence to some of the other means of obtaining compliance.

1. The *ex officio* institution "authority": the right of office-holders to order, and the duty of those subject to their authority to comply. (This defines the legal aspect of authority.)

2. The *de facto* relation: the effective exercise of authority by the officials vested with it, and acceptance by those subject to it.[22] (This defines authority as a consensual social relationship which links citizens to their leaders and thereby to each other.)

3. Power: the ability to compel others to comply with one's wishes, regardless of authority.

4. Influence: the ability to make others acquiesce (by persuasion, prestige, or loyalty) without relying altogether on *de jure*

22. The decline of authority (p. 120).

authority or on actual power. (Influence is not far from *de facto* authority but need not be exercised by officeholders.)

5. Violence: physical force used by a person, directly or through a weapon, to hurt, destroy, or control another or to damage, destroy, or control an object (e.g., territory or property). Violence can be used for the acquisition and exercise of power and to challenge authority or to enforce it. I shall focus on these political uses of violence.

Force and Violence

The social meanings of physically identical actions often are distinguished verbally. Thus, physical force is called "force" when authorized and regarded as legitimate, and "violence" otherwise: the arresting officer employs force, the resisting suspect, violence. However, the nouns appear to imply, and thus a priori to decide, what is yet to be shown. Therefore, I prefer to use "violence" as synonym for physical "force" and when necessary to qualify it as legitimate or illegitimate. The adjectival, which thus replaces the substantive distinction, is more easily perceived as separately normative; the moral legitimacy of force is clearly seen to depend on whether one considers an authority (and its use of force) as legitimate, or so regards the force used to challenge it.

Violence and Violation

"Violence" (from the Latin *violentia*) is an act of physical force which may but need not violate a norm as well. "Violation" (from the Latin *violatio*) does not require violence. Fraud violates legal and moral norms but does not use violence. Assault uses violence and violates norms. Finally, subduing a fugitive criminal may call for violence but need not violate any norm.

Because acts of physical force frequently do violate norms or, at least, expectations, the meaning of "violence" is often conflated with that of "violation." Grievous violations are referred to as violence (as in "he did violence to") and violent acts are called violations (as in "he violated her"). This conflation has lured some theoreticians into referring to violations of their standards of justice as "violence" even when no force is used. Such an extension of the meaning of "violence" makes it hard to distinguish unjust physical force from violations which occur without physical force, such as unjust deprivation. Writers who refuse to acknowledge this distinction claim that there is no difference, but their claim "does violence to" the facts.

Additional Meanings of Violence

An intense feeling, a contrast, or a massive physical event, such as a storm or an accidental death, all may be called violent on occasion. Any excessive, strong, or merely abrupt or external force which violates expectations, if not norms, may be called violent. But this "violence" need not concern us, since it is connected with the political use of force only by irrelevant analogy.

Uses of Violence

Human violence which in the main refers to past actions of those on whom it is inflicted is punitive or (when regarded as illegitimate) vindictive. Violence which mainly discharges present emotions is expressive, and violence instrumentally used to acquire things valued (other than power or prestige) is acquisitive. Violence used to acquire, extend, or retain power or authority is political. Counterviolence is defensive and may be deterrent or retaliatory as well.

Persons and Property

The law distinguishes violence against persons (assault) from violence against things. This distinction is of little relevance to political analysis, concerned more with violence as an instrument of coercion than with the kind or severity of the injuries or damages inflicted. Moreover, political violence cannot easily separate things from persons: if one breaks into an office, blows up a laboratory, or storms the Winter Palace, and still more, if one defends any of these places, the force used tends to injure people as well as damage things.

Nonviolence

Violence against lawful activities or authorities is unlawful. So are some nonviolent actions such as civil disobedience and disruption, sit-ins, illicit occupation of sites and buildings, expulsion or sequestration of persons. Such actions require no violence, as long as they are tolerated by those affected. But if their influence proves unavailing, law enforcement agencies, and the persons interfered with, either must suffer nonviolent unlawful actions or halt them by force. While they thus may invite it, nonviolent offenders need not initiate any violence of their own; they may not even resist violently when force is used against them.

Although precarious in fact and dubious in morality, the distinction between violent and nonviolent law violation is important to politics in theory and practice. Nonviolent defiance illustrates the difference between "violence" and "violation"—and the usefulness of verbally distinguishing nonviolent norm or law violations, whether by an authority or by its opponents, from violence.

The thrust of nonviolent defiance is suasive. Authority is challenged and legal norms are violated to draw attention to the claim that the authority itself violates norms morally more important than those defied and to persuade people to resist lawful orders thought to violate moral norms. Nonviolence seldom attempts to coerce authority otherwise or to overthrow it.

In contrast, violent defiance tends to be intimidatory, expressive, punitive, or outright coercive. Violence seldom can produce popular support, although it may incidentally reduce (or enlarge) it. While nonviolence tries to produce assent, violence tries to coerce; it succeeds only when sufficient support already exists or when reactions are inept enough to produce it.

Because it is an important alternative means of political action, nonviolence should not be omitted altogether from the study of political violence. More saliently, nonviolent law violation shifts the political burden of resorting to violence to the parties defied.

Authority, Force and Credibility

Law violations are most persuasive when those defied by them either exclude resort to violence, or use it ineptly, or irresolutely: prematurely, tardily, too much, too little, against too many or too few, on the wrong issue, or against the wrong persons.[*] Any mishandling of violence reduces the acceptability of authority, whether the mishandling appears to condone the violation of norms (e.g., irresolution) or itself appears to violate norms (e.g., excessive or premature force).

Authority remains effective when its instructions are obeyed without violence, but can be enforced, if need be, by using violence without discrediting the authority. Misuse, unwarranted use, above all, unwarranted nonuse, make force appear illegitimate as an instrument of authority. So does precipitate, tardy, insufficient, or incoherent use. The authority which uses it so ineptly as to make force appear illegitimate deprives itself of acceptability. It loses effectiveness, and ultimately its moral legitimacy as well. Shorn of credibility in the minds of the governed, authority is discredited, bereft of moral and, ultimately, of material power. Violent contests may follow, until a new, or renewed, authority is credible enough to be accepted.

Credibility, then, is a necessary element in the *de facto* authority relationship. But not sufficient: moral acceptability is required as well. It is provided by tradition, ideological justifications, and faith. Proportions vary. But some degree of faith and perceived ideological justifiability is indispensable to moral acceptability. Authority must be regarded as just by those who are to accept it.

Where authority and influence do not suffice to determine or,

[*] "Wrong" here means so as to increase support for those against whom violence is used, thereby strengthening rather than weakening their political effectiveness.

at least, limit conduct, violence tends to be used either to reinforce authority, or to oppose it, or to achieve individual ends independent of it. Yet violence leads to enduring social power only if wielded by leaders of groups. Leaders are leaders inasmuch as they have *de facto* authority (moral acceptability and credibility) over the group they lead. Hence authority can never be wholly replaced by violence or power.

The Chinese Communist leader Mao Tse-tung who said, "Power grows out of the barrel of a gun," stated a necessary but not sufficient condition for social power. For guns must be in the hands of people who accept the authority of their leaders. The *bon mot* of the nineteenth-century Italian leader Cavour, "One can do anything with bayonets except sit on them," suggests that consensual authority is indispensable to social power.

What occasionally looks like disappearance of authority is a redistribution usually associated with temporary disorder and sporadic violence. Violence is conspicuous also where the *de facto* authority of one group ends (e.g., that of the police), while the power of another (e.g., that of the Mafia or of the Black Panthers) is not fully established.

Although it can be a temporary alternative, force is not inconsistent with nor wholly separate from authority, any more than it is identical with it.[23] It is a supplement which even the most accepted authority must sometimes use and, above all, always be ready to use. Ineffective authority must resort frequently to force to replace insufficient acceptance. And when violence is used against it, authority obviously has been insufficient to make the user refrain. Often, but not always, it can be reestablished by using superior force.

23. The penumbra of authority (p. 120).

Violence and Other Means of Coercion

Political and Nonpolitical Violence

Never less than physical force, violence is coercive only when used instrumentally to control the future actions of people; it is politically so when used to control or influence collective policies or the distribution of power. Violence by individuals is political only when it has such social aims. However, group violence is always political in effect, whatever the motivations of the participants: it necessarily has political reverberations. Riots, therefore, are political violence, even though the motives are as often vindictive, acquisitive, or expressive, as they are coercive and political.

Although both may be reactions to the politically sanctioned social order, political differs from nonpolitical violence. The latter has no social aims, while political violence directly addresses social policies or power distributions or the social order as a whole. Nonpolitical violence, however much conditioned by the politically sanctioned social context, does not address it deliberately. It is the effect sought (or achieved) which distinguishes political from nonpolitical violence, not the causes from which either springs. Even when legal punishment is politically distributed (i.e., unjustly and with political bias), the punishment does not make the acts for which it is inflicted "political," nor the actors, unless their acts were attempts to change the political order. Political penalization generates victims or beneficiaries of politics. It cannot retroactively generate political acts or actors.

War

Intergovernmental violence—war—is exquisitely political: violence used for political coercion by law-making—but not law-ruled—sovereigns through specialized organizations (the military). But the violence of lawmakers against each other differs in important respects from violence among citizens ruled by law and from violence between citizens and their government. Intergovernmental violence rests on Jean Bodin's *potestas legibus absoluta* (power not dependent on law) of sovereigns (much as we might wish otherwise)—on the absence (actual if not conceptual) of sanctioned legal regulation of relations among sovereigns. In contrast, intragovernmental violence occurs within, despite, and sometimes against a legal order sanctioned by a political authority which regulates relations among citizens and between them and their government.

Domestically, force is always legally restricted and not allowed to decide conflicts among citizens. But among sovereign governments, and certainly in war, law distributes the right to the use of violence quite generously. Even though the law attempts to impose some limits, violence ultimately decides intergovernmental conflicts but not intragovernmental ones. Because the difference between domestic and intergovernmental violence is so great, discussion of war has to be omitted here.[24]

24. War and legality (p. 120).

Coercive Force and Coercion by Force

Locutions such as "force of circumstances" or "he is forced to . . ." can be confusing because they do not separate (internal) compulsion from (external) coercion. Worse, such locutions do not discriminate between violence and other means of coercion —between *coercion by force* (violence) and *coercive force* (pressure not necessarily violence). The distinction is essential to political analysis.

The use of violence for coercion has already been separated from other uses of violence. We must now distinguish violence from other means of coercion. Instruments of coercion do not become identical because they all are coercive any more than foods become identical because they all are nutritive or edible. The *genus* is the same but there remains a *differentia:* violence surely differs from other means of coercion such as deprivation. It should hardly be necessary to add that coercion, whatever the means, differs from inducement, as the carrot does from the stick, though the results be identical.

Coercion

Coercion is an avoidable external process deliberately inflicted to restrict, tilt, or deform the victim's range of discretion so as to exclude some of his choices or to impose one's own. Coercion is mild when confined to the exclusion of choices, the milder the more acceptable the exclusions. Coercion is strong if choices are imposed, the stronger the less acceptable the imposed choices are to the victim. Coercion is the process of excluding or imposing choices. The results achieved by the process—be they death, poverty, or pregnancy—are seldom called coercion.

Restriction

Coercion entails restriction. But restriction of choice need not entail coercion or be caused by it. The robber who restricts choice to "your money or your life" does coerce his victim: he intentionally inflicts an avoidable restriction. But having less money than Mr. Rockefeller, though it restricts, does not coerce me. There has been no externally inflicted, avoidable process intended to deprive me, to deliberately restrict my choices, or to impose those of others. To be sure extreme poverty is extremely restrictive and, therefore, a hardship. But the restriction, or deprivation, however hard to bear, is not a coercion unless it is avoidable and intentionally inflicted. Even then, only the process of infliction is called coercion.

Violence, Hardship and Coercion

Violence is one of many means that can be used for coercion. So is, of course, the credible threat of violence. Other hardships are usable for coercion too. Detention may be used deliberately to control present or future actions, e.g., by holding a person for ransom. More often, detention is used merely for punishment of past actions. The anticipation of punishment is coercive but punishment itself seldom controls future actions. (Note that holding for ranson is coercive but not a punishment.) Whether coercive or not, detention is not violence, although force may be used to impose it. Indeed, violence may be used against a prisoner separately and, additionally, for vindictive or coercive purposes. So with poverty, another hardship. Detention deprives of freedom, poverty of comforts. Both can be used for coercion. Both can be the result of coercion. But neither need be. Finally, force can be used as an instrument to inflict most hardships. But it differs significantly from the hardships it can be used to inflict, such as poverty or imprisonment.

Poverty as an Effect

The victim of violence and the victim of poverty both suffer; both are restricted; and both may, but need not be coerced by what victimizes them. But unlike violence, poverty (or even hunger) is rarely used instrumentally. It is most frequently the outcome of ineptness, governmental or individual; occasionally it is the effect of natural or historical circumstances but seldom of deliberate privation inflicted to coerce.* A quite different matter may be argued plausibly: poverty can be the effect of circumstances inflicted *by* but not *for* coercion. If so, the coercion which results in poverty is rarely intended to produce the result it does not avoid.

If, however, victims were made to suffer hunger for the sake of coercing them, the effects, including their choices, would differ from those produced by violence. The victim whose poverty is used for coercion may prefer misery or starvation to undesired sex. But the victim of violence may not have this choice. The victim of poverty may become additionally a victim of violence, while the victim of violence need not be poor at all.

Poverty as "Violence against the Poor"

Restriction often is confused with coercion, and so is violent with nonviolent coercion. Thus, at least in the minds of the more passionate theoreticians of poverty and of violence (though not

---

* Ineptness seems to explain more realistically hunger among American Indians and in India, than any policy intended to produce privation, let alone one that uses privation for coercive purposes.

of the victims of either) poverty becomes "violence against the poor." However, to proclaim poverty "institutional violence" is to do violence to actuality, by calling "violence" whatever violation one is opposed to—a confused way of registering one's disapproval. Some, however, argue seriously that since the social order, including the social structure (the distribution of inequalities), is ultimately enforced by violence, violence enforces every position granted or imposed by the social order, including poverty. Hence poverty is "violence against the poor."

This argument proves not what it means to prove—that the social order is intended and enforced to keep some people poor —but merely that the social order is enforced. The social order secures every lawful condition or activity, not only that of the poor. Anyone who tries to change his position or to interfere with anyone else's by violating a social rule is coerced not to do so—whether he be a poor person trying to escape poverty, or a rich one attempting to get richer, or someone beating his wife. Hence it is correct to say that a social order coerces, if need be by violence, all those who try to violate its rules. But it is incorrect to single out the rules to which one attributes poverty. Being poor is neither necessary nor sufficient for the violation of rules or for their enforcement.

Coercion and, when necessary, force must be used against those who, for whatsoever reason, violate the rules of any social order—even of an ideally just or egalitarian one. Else it would not be an order.* Perhaps ideal orders have to use force against fewer discontented persons. But unless true by definition, this is doubtful. That a social order is enforced by violence and results in disadvantages to some, such as poverty, does not justify calling these disadvantages, or the order, "violence." Even though they are enforced by violence against violators (who may well become violators because placed at a disadvantage) traffic rules are not usually described as violence against drivers or pedestrians. Nor is traffic. Yet drivers who have compelling reasons to

* See pp. 13–18.

hurry must stop at the red light with drivers who can easily afford to stop—just as the disadvantaged must refrain from violating laws together with persons who can more easily afford to be law-abiding. Thus, to say, "Poverty is violence against the poor," is either wrong or a misleading way of saying that poverty is a violation of one's standards of justice—an odd mode of expressing the true (if unsurprising) notion that to be poor is to suffer the disadvantages of poverty.

Violence is a physical act whether it breaks or enforces a rule, just or unjust. Violence is not a position or condition of advantage or disadvantage, such as being alive or dead, rich or poor, just or unjust. Some of these conditions can be attained, retained, or changed by force. But the force so used must not be confused with the condition it produces, retains, or changes. Thus, if A shoots B, A uses violence, however just the reason. If B's life was protected by law, that law, however unjust, is not an act of violence, though enforced by acts of violence. If A does the shooting because he suffers poverty, his condition is not violence though his act is (and either may be unjust).

Inequality, Justice and Violence

In all societies some people have more advantages (wealth, income, power, prestige) than others. The institutional rules, on which distribution of advantages depends, differ from society to society and are part of the social order. Together with people's ability to utilize them, these rules or institutions produce the result: the position of each person within the society, "rich" or "poor," and the degree and kind of social equality or inequality. All or some of these may be perceived as violations of rules of justice.

Any social order, finally, is enforced by a combination of authority and violence. The proportions depend largely on the degree of consent. However social consent is not the same as social justice as seen by an ideal outsider. A social order with immense inequalities, and in which positions are entirely ascribed at birth— e.g., a caste system—conceivably may be consented to more and may be enforced by less violence than a more egalitarian order in which positions are achieved by individual effort. Yet it is the latter that, at least since the eighteenth century, would appear more just. Consent depends on justice only as perceived within the social order.

Is the Burden of Violence Shifted?

It can be argued that nonviolent restrictions, such as poverty, place the burden of violence on the poor who are unwilling to be restricted by them, just as nonviolent law defiance shifts the burden of violence on those unwilling to suffer the defiance. But unlike nonviolent law defiance, poverty is (1) not a (nonviolent or violent) illegal act against the poor, which authorizes or requires their violence in defense of their legal rights; (2) not intentionally used as a means to coerce or to deprive the poor; (3) poverty is not caused by those to whom the violence of the poor is to be addressed; they do not control the means which create or remedy poverty; (4) poverty is remediable, if at all, by means other than violence and is seldom effectively cured by it.

As is location or tradition or religion, poverty (or wealth) is among inducements and restrictions in the choice of activities. But these are neither coercions nor violence.* The poverty of the poor is not the intent, or the effect, of the wealth or wickedness of the rich (or of the "system") any more than disease need be the effect of health or be inflicted by the healthy on the sick. Other causes account for poverty and disease.

* The difference between the inducements and restrictions of a market system and the coercions of a nonmarket system is patent to anyone who compares the market system with a military or penal one.

Poverty and Oppression

A social order which deliberately places some people at an unwarranted and avoidable disadvantage and does not allow them to participate in decisions which affect them oppresses the disadvantaged.* When used against oppression, violence can be justified and effective as a remedy. But poverty seldom is caused by oppression and, therefore, seldom remedied by violence. Nor is poverty proof of oppression which can be detected independently.**

Governments, Poverty and Disease

Hunger, disease, poverty, or other diffusely restrictive circumstances can be controlled by political authority only sometimes, partially, and usually indirectly. Often the means to control hunger (food) or disease (cure) are not available at all, or insufficient. Even when governments can produce hospitals, they do not necessarily produce cures. The ability of the government to foster production of effective remedies (and therefore its obligation: *ultra posse nemo obligatur*)*** is limited. The distribution of the means available can be controlled by governments only to some extent. Often the morally preferred equitable distribution of food or medical care is inconsistent with the needed quantitative and qualitative maximization of production. Even

* There is a large evaluative element in "unwarranted" and a small one in "avoidable."

** The *relative* poverty of American blacks is probably the partial result of *past* oppression, but the poverty of American whites cannot be so explained, nor that of African blacks or of Chinese, Egyptian, or Polish peasants.

*** Nobody can be obligated beyond his ability.

when the government can optimize production and distribution of food and medical care, malnutrition or disease need not be minimized, for they do not altogether depend on what the government makes available: people cannot easily be compelled (and few would argue that they should be) to take the available medicines, to earn a living (given the opportunity), to eat healthy foods, or to refrain from unhealthy behavior such as smoking, or driving, let alone racing.*

Governments can monopolize violence, and force people to refrain from it with a reasonable degree of success, to advantage, and without major drawbacks. Most other evils or goods are harder to control. It will help if, before returning to violence, we disentangle what governments can and cannot control. Society is often blamed for evils beyond its power to affect and for others which it could not correct without creating worse ones. The dissatisfaction thus misdirected against it is a major source of violence against and in defense of the social order.

Rights, Abilities, Opportunities

Rights and Governments

Legal rights and immunities are limited to matters the government has the power to grant and distribute. Other things, such as loneliness, love, violent toothaches, hunger, or God's grace, often are more important to people. Governments do not control most of these. Oliver Goldsmith's view remains true, although

* See Nathan Glazer, "Paradoxes of Health Care," *The Public Interest* (Winter 1971).

most sociologists (and all bureaucrats) are reluctant to take it seriously:

> How small, of all that human hearts endure,
> The part which laws or kings can cause or cure.

Perhaps one should amend this: "laws and kings" can "cause" much and "cure" little. Further, the character of a society, culture, as distinguished from government, does affect individuals ("human hearts") in a major way. But attempts to deliberately extend direct government control over culture are likely to be costly and ineffective, and disastrous if effective. (Independent, noncoercive efforts to affect culture need not be. They may be fostered by governments.)

Confusion between what is within the government's power and what, though vastly more important, is not, often leads to fervid demands that the government grant what is not in its power to grant. People crave not leave to pursue happiness—freedom—which the government can give, but happiness itself, which only God can grant.[25]

Four Freedoms

Franklin Delano Roosevelt's "four freedoms" illustrate the confusion at issue. (I shall use this as a paradigm.) FDR ignored the obviously limited ability of any government to grant freedom from want or disease.[26] He also confused health, or affluence, with freedom. But the absence of disease or want is a state or an ability, not a freedom. A healthy or wealthy person can be enslaved (some of the inmates of German concentration camps were wealthy), and a sick (or hungry) person free. And health or affluence seldom can be granted by the government, at least not to most persons. To be rid of disease or want is to be healthy or wealthy,

25. Dostoyevsky on happiness (p. 121).
26. FDR's "freedoms from . . ." (p. 121).

and thus able to do what one is unable to do when not, to *use* one's freedom and to *exercise* one's rights (e.g., to travel, earn money, or make love). The rights are granted by the government. The state of health, or wealth, and the ability conferred thereby is neither a right nor a freedom. Rights and freedoms are what the government can do about permitting or entitling us to use abilities which are "granted" by God, or nature, or produced by a combination of nature, social opportunity, accident, and individual endeavors.

Abilities and Rights

Governments can influence whatever induces, compels, or prevents people from exercising the rights which governments actually can grant. But governments cannot altogether control the (largely exogenous) opportunities, and the (largely endogenous) abilities to eat, or travel, or work, or be healthy, regardless of whether they be "socially" or "naturally" acquired (inborn).[27] Nonetheless, the right to marry, to choose spouses, or to stay single is valuable—even when the government does not supply or distribute the ability or the spouses. The right to live, travel, drink, and be merry remains valuable, even if your age, mood, illnesses, principles, or lack of money prevent you from utilizing it. And so with all rights, however unequally distributed the abilities and the conditions which make their exercise possible, desirable, or compelling.

Anatole France on Rights

The confusion between rights totally dependent on the government and conditions which, at best, are only partially within its control is well exemplified by Anatole France's attempt to

27. Social and natural matters (p. 121).

ridicule "the law [which] in its majestic equality forbids rich and poor alike to sleep under bridges . . . and to steal bread." Laws indeed do impose the same prohibition on people living in conditions so different, owing to their different social locations, that the prohibition will be totally irrelevant to some and vitally important to others.* But such laws are unjust only if unnecessarily imposed on people forced to violate them because no legitimate alternative is available to them. And rights lose their value only if the inability to utilize them is total and permanent, so as to be unresponsive to all lawful action within the control of those affected. This is not the case of poverty in a democratic capitalist system. (In contrast, a caste system, or a totalitarian one, might not grant the rights to be exercised or, if it does grant them, may altogether preclude opportunities for their exercise by some groups.)

It is highly misleading to identify the attempts of governments to improve or equalize (quite different matters) people's abilities or their opportunities, however desirable, with a grant of rights. Only the government can grant rights—whereas the government is never the only possible source of conditions and abilities, always a limited one and seldom the best.[28]

Confusions: Marcuse and Others

The confusion between freedom (governmental leave), rights (entitlements), and immunities (protection), and, on the other hand, one's ability to use any of these, or finally, the conditions which make such use possible, desirable, or necessary reaches far. By describing the failure of the government to grant what it does not control as "institutional violence," those who foster this confusion attempt to justify what they describe as "reactive" violence against the government. Herbert Marcuse's refusal to distinguish

* The analogy to traffic rules noted above (pp. 65–66) is pertinent here.
28. Liberté, egalité, fraternité (p. 122).

between coercion by violence and by deprivation demonstrates how confused confusion can get—in the right hands.* Marcuse first confuses restriction with coercion; and then, unbelievably, he confuses coercion with influence and with inducement by affluence and all of these with violence.

Although perhaps more candid than others, Herbert Marcuse is not alone in redefining violence so as to make it, in Christian Bay's words, "useful for underdog interests."** Professor Bay simply defines violence as "any cause of needless reduction in basic freedoms for any human being" (at best a violation) and endorses John Galtung's definition of violence as "the cause of the difference . . . between what could have been and what is."*** Either definition would make any "needless" coercion, or restriction and any deprivation "violence." This is a "needless" confusion. The purpose of a definition is to make it possible to refer to different things by different words. And surely a man who is needlessly deprived of freedom—e.g., not allowed to say or read something or to travel somewhere—is not being assaulted? If both things are harmful they cause different harms by different means. If both reduce freedom they do reduce different freedoms by different means. Surely not all harmful actions are "violence"? Is the nonattainment of attainable benefits (Galtung's definition of "violence") always due to "violence" and never to differences of opinion on what should be attained and how, or to indolence?

Similarly Bernard Harrison insists that "structural injustice" in a legal system can justify violence since, by definition, it is injurious and may not permit any other resort to the injured.† This is true, if not original. But Mr. Harrison goes on to be original, if

---

* For a fullbodied and incisive history of "freedom from" and "freedom to" see Sir Isaiah Berlin's *Four Essays on Liberty* (Oxford, 1969). For Herbert Marcuse see *A Critique of Pure Tolerance* (Beacon, 1970), particularly pp. 100, 101, 105–107, 118 ff.

** "A Liberation of Violence," *The American Scholar* (October 1971).

*** Ibid.

† "Violence and the Role of Law," in *Violence,* Jerome A. Shaffer, ed. (New York: David McKay, 1971).

not true. He argues that since no society is ideal (i.e., can avoid structural injustice) violence is always justifiable unless society, by negotiation, does what those who feel injured by "structural injustice" want.* This argument, willfully or naively, obliterates the difference between societies that have mechanisms to correct (or, pessimistically, to change) structural injustices, such as democracy, and those which do not. Neither society is, or can become, perfect. But the former does not require violence for change, while the latter does. Failure to correct what some feel to be an injustice cannot justify violence unless (a) the injustice is demonstrable and (b) can be shown to be correctible by feasible violence and not otherwise, without (c) producing worse injustice. Whether or not actually corrected in a democracy injustice is nearly always correctible without violence.**

Violence, Order and Justice

The coercive use of actual violence has been a government prerogative since time immemorial. It must be. Without monopolizing violence, no government can effectively grant any rights or attempt to foster the production, or a preferred distribution, of the conditions or opportunities needed to exercise the rights granted. The *raison d'être,* the paramount duty and the defining characteristic of governments is, therefore, the attempt to monopolize violence and to declare any nonauthorized use of it to be illegitimate. It is by thus restricting violence that governments provide security for the citizens in their lawful pursuits and are able to grant effective liberties, rights and immunities, and even, within limits, to foster and distribute the ability and opportunity to use them.

"Justice" is an ideal order, preferred to others. The order en-

* "Structural injustice" may be unavoidable by definition so that societies may differ only in their distribution of it.

** For qualifications (which seem, however, irrelevant to Mr. Harrison's argument as I understand it) see pp. 23–26.

forced by any government through its monopoly of authorized violence may not be just enough in the opinion of those who wish to change it. Justice is more than "law and order." But it cannot be less: a just order still is an order enforced by law. The desire for a just order raises the moral question: when and how is violence against the government justified? Obviously violence against the government is always illegal. But unless one holds with Thomas Hobbes that "the laws are the rules of just and unjust," wherefore "no law can be unjust," what is legal need not be moral. One may question whether, and when, he is morally free, or even obligated, to use violence against a government, and what violence the government is morally free, or obligated, to use. In addition to questions of justification, there are problems of explanation: what causes antigovernmental violence and what makes it effective? What causes the use of effective or ineffective counterviolence?

Justifications of Violence

Since it is potentially most injurious to individuals and to the body politic, violence is justifiable only when its ends cannot be attained by other less costly means and when the ends can justify the cost. Few ends do.

Violence and Democracy

In a democracy violence is needed, and therefore justifiable, only if one despairs of the far less costly process of persuading the majority, yet believes a change of policy to be important enough to impose it without majority support.* For, if it can be produced, majority support would bring about policy changes in a less costly way by elections. A democratic government can be ousted freely, legally, and without violence when opposed by the majority. Since violence is needed only when its aims are not supported by the majority, the cost of violence against a democratic government includes the cost of forcefully imposing policies not approved, or opposed by the majority. Such policies can be imposed at length only by a government which, since it is opposed by the majority, cannot be democratic. It must be kept in power by force used against the majority. At the least, citizens must be shorn of the civil rights which they would use to oust the nondemocratic government and to reinstate the policies they prefer.

The cost of violence against a democratic government thus equals the cost of the injuries inflicted plus (if the violence is successful) the cost of minority dictatorship. Justification requires that the benefits exceed these costs: the benefit of the policy change opposed by the majority must exceed the cost of imposing and continuing minority dictatorship.

Marxist Views

Marxists (other than democratic Marxists—almost an oxymoron) used to face this result, although not unambiguously. They advocated "the dictatorship of the proletariat." The idea has not changed. Euphemisms have, but only a little. Whence Herbert Marcuse advocates "the dictatorship of an elite over the people" and the disenfranchisement of all those who do not share the historically, or morally, correct views—his—because they were misconditioned by capitalism.** (They must have been: to Mar-

* See pp. 19–21 and *passim*.
** See Marcuse, *A Critique of Pure Tolerance,* pp. 100 and 120.

cuse there can be no other explanation for the failure of the "masses" to share his views. Although incautiously formulated, his idea is Marxian.)

We are to be saved from our mistaken ambitions—ambitions that capitalism unnaturally injected into us—if need be by the scruff of our collective neck: "the slaves must be forced to be free."* Marcuse's followers do not explain what enables them— them alone—to transcend capitalist conditioning; nor who will decide who has. How can we tell those who should from those who should not be part of the elite by a criterion other than agreement or disagreement with Marcuse? The dire fate of many Soviet, Cuban, Chinese, and even Yugoslav Marxists (let alone anti-Marxists, peasants or workers) seems too inauspicious, and too ominous, to ignore.

Left and Right Elitism

The Fascist or Nazi "right" used to hold elitist convictions with as much self-righteously impassioned fervor as the "left" does now. They, the elite of the nation (just as the vanguard of the proletariat), or of the race, or of humanity were to save us all. For the purpose, people, however reluctant owing to misconditioning (what else could it be?), had to be pushed into revolution violently, if necessary: dictatorship was to be our salvation.

The defeat of Nazis and Fascists has had a sobering effect. So did the ensuing revelations of their cruelty, corruption, stupidity and inefficiency. Today few rightists will accept the elitist claims of Fascists or Nazis. But too little has been understood as yet about the delusions which produced their initial success. A new generation of leftists seems condemned to repeat the history of the right which it ignores.

---

* Here Marcuse paraphrases (without acknowledgment) the worst moments of a far more subtle thinker: J. J. Rousseau.

The publication after Stalin's death of what had been obvious to those who cared to see had some sobering effects on the left, as did the subsequent invasion of Hungary and again, that of Czechoslovakia by the post-Stalin and the post-Khrushchev Soviet Union. But sobriety proved temporary, perhaps because the dictatorships which use leftist ideologies and symbols never were defeated in war, unlike those which used rightist ideologies and symbols. On the contrary, leftist dictatorships were able to expand. Hence leftist symbols and slogans, although a little shopworn, have not lost their charm. In leftist eyes Stalin is discredited, but communist dictatorships such as Mao's or Castro's are not. "Excesses" are attributed to Stalin's mistakes—not to the unchecked opportunities for cruelty and stupidity any totalitarian dictatorship necessarily offers.*

"Formal" and "True" Democracy

The slogans still, or again, used to justify the violent overthrow of the democratic in favor of a vaguely more free and equal and socialist form of government claim that the "formal" democracy to be overthrown is not "true" or "substantive" democracy, which alone redeems the essential democratic promise of welfare, security, peace, freedom, justice, and equality. We have none of these, it is claimed. Therefore "formal" democracy has failed and is not worth defending, being of little value, particularly to the working class. Since people have been deluded into thinking otherwise, they must be freed from this delusion by violence and regardless of their expressed wishes, if need be. Above all, people must be freed from the conditions—"formal" democracy and capitalism—which produce delusions and wishes in them contrary

---

* The most factual account of Stalin's "excesses," of the killing of more than twenty million people in Russian concentration camps, is found in Robert Conquest's *The Great Terror* (Macmillan, 1968).

to their true interests. Once freed they will voluntarily submit to the elite which freed them and which, therefore, will no longer have to impose its will. Let us consider this claim.

"Formal" democracy rests on normative axiomatic definitional qualities and on substantive propositions. The latter are empirical predictions, helpful in justifying democracy, but not indispensable to the definition. (1) An axiom: citizens ought to govern themselves, however well or badly they do it (the last must be stressed: *even when they do so badly*). Self-government is never less than the right of the citizens, institutionally provided for, of freely electing and ousting their governments. This right is what makes democracy democratic.* (2) A proposition: when citizens can freely elect and oust governments by majority (as is the case in the U.S.) they come about as near to self-government as is feasible in a modern (urbanized, industrial, populous) society. (3) An axiom: the political freedom (civil rights) which citizens must have to elect and oust governments is also valuable *per se*. (4) A proposition: once a democracy is established at length, it tends to extend the franchise and ultimately to include all adults in the political process; it enlarges as well the nonpolitical freedoms of the citizens. It is likely to increase their welfare, since it allows them to control the government.

Historical experience suggests that "formal" democracy is entirely compatible with misgovernment, corruption, injustice, inefficiency, immorality, unrepresentativeness (at least in Arrow's sense**), cultural and aesthetic infertility and with sociopsychological unwisdom. So is every other political system.[29] It is even conceivable that enlargement of freedom is inconsistent with increases of welfare and that when either or both go beyond a

* To elect and oust "freely" is to have the "civil liberties" required for the formation of diverse opinions and independent political groups which freely select candidates for office.
** See Fn. 12 (p. 112).
29. Ideal and actual systems (p. 122).

certain point, they have destabilizing effects. (This possibility has not been sufficiently investigated despite its overwhelming relevance to contemporary problems. Is there such a critical point? Can we locate it? Are we unavoidably impelled to go beyond it?)

"Formal" and "True" Democracy Compared

Compared to the alternatives, "formal" democracy has the (intrinsic) advantages of its normative axioms and also the (extrinsic) advantage of greater substantive benefits. Its empirical propositions vouchsafe that in the long run "formal" democracy is more apt to lead to peace, justice and welfare than systems which promise these benefits at the expense of self-government and of freedom.

1. The leaders and governments of a democracy, although not often better, seldom are worse than the voters who elect them. This is a modest claim. Nonetheless, it is important. Dictators such as Hitler and Stalin surely were worse than their subjects. Germans and Russians could be dictated to by evil madmen because citizens were bereft of the right freely to oust their governments by vote, or to oppose it peacefully. In democracies citizens are further protected from mistreatment, which is routine in dictatorships, because the authority and the power of democratic leaders is more limited than the authority and the power of dictators.

2. Since the citizens of a "formal" democracy usually want the substantive benefits attributed to "true" democracy, democratic governments tend to move toward these benefits. They must, since they depend on the consent and support of the citizens. There is no reason why "formal" democracies should be less successful in approaching these benefits than dictatorships ("true"

democracies). Democratic claims are likely to be less hyperbolic only because they can be verified (or disconfirmed) by institutions independent of the government and, ultimately, by the voters.

3. There is nothing in the nature of "formal" democracy to prevent its combination with whatever substantive social or economic reforms—socialist or otherwise—the citizens decide they want. On the other hand, nondemocratic systems almost necessarily lose the benefits for the sake of which they are instituted. They degenerate: since it can not be ousted legitimately, the governing group becomes independent of those whom it governs and tends to benefit itself more than them.

Freedom: The Right to Be Right—and Also to Be Wrong?

Advocates of the violent overthrow of "formal" in favor of "true" democracy insist that in formal democracy "the masses" are not actually able to use their franchise for their benefit. The evidence offered is that "the masses" are not as well off as they would be, in the opinion of their mentors, if they actually were able to use "formal" democracy for their benefit. Their inability is produced by capitalist conditioning of their attitudes. Else, they would vote, and act, as good Marxists feel they ought to. The implication is that people are not truly free in "formal" democracy as long as they are not socialists. Evidence of freedom does not consist of absence of restraints, but of desirable results: free people do what I regard as good; if they do not, they are not truly free. At the least, they must have been misled.

Freedom, then, is not freedom to err, to suffer from one's mistakes, and to benefit from one's wisdom; it is "freedom" only when errors are avoided and benefits achieved. In the words of the German philosopher Johann Gottlieb Fichte, "no one has . . . rights against reason."

Alienation

People would not be misled into wrong ambitions and policies were it not for capitalist institutions which condition them so perversely that they become alienated from proper gratification of their own "human needs," from their true and good nature. They become unable even to perceive what policies would benefit them. Because people cannot be truly free under capitalism, their political decisions cannot be truly theirs. Since they never had "true" freedom—the "freedom"(?) to do not what they want but what they ought to want—and since the advocates of "true" democracy know better what people need than they do, nothing is lost when people's "formal" freedom is replaced by Marcuse's "dictatorship of the elite." Fichte, from whom Marcuse took more than he knows or cares to admit, put it clearly: "to compel men to adopt the right form of government, to impose right on them by force . . . is the sacred duty of every man who has both the insight and the power to do so." (So far, those who think as Marcuse does only have the "insight"—which may be just as well.)[30]

Rape, Seduction and Mass Media

There is nothing new in the contention of Marcuse and his followers that capitalism deprives people of "freedom" (as defined in his rather free manner), since it somehow makes people want what Marcuse thinks is wrong. There are, however, two politically new elements in the "New Left" which he pioneered. First

30. Positive and negative freedom (p. 122).

the stress on (pseudo-Freudian) psychological factors. Money, it has been discovered, isn't everything; even if you have it, capitalism alienates you. And second, the stress on the seductive effect of mass media. (There are anarchist elements as well, but they are not new.)

With respect to the mass media and to political processes, seduction (a disapproved influence) is conceived as though rape (coercion by violence). The distinction between persuasion and violence is basic to democracy. Democracy permits persuasion but outlaws violence, while dictatorship outlaws both. If they are indistinguishable then, indeed, both must be outlawed. Meanwhile the equivocation helps justify violence: if there is no difference between rape and seduction . . . might as well.

Yet the confusion is widespread, particularly among the young. Thus the Cox Commission Report about violence at Columbia University quotes an anonymous student as saying: "direct action . . . sit-ins and . . . physical violence . . . are political tools fairly comparable to the large political contribution, lobbying, favoritism, cocktail parties . . . used by the establishment."

Now, it is true that cocktail-party persuasion, used by the establishment, may achieve the same results as a "confrontation" used by its opponents. It does not follow that one "political tool" is as legitimate as the other. Even though rape may achieve the same result as seduction, it does not become legitimate therefore. Persuasion (and seduction) at cocktail parties, or elsewhere, involves voluntary compliance of those influenced by it. Rape (or "confrontation") compels (or attempts to compel) the victim to comply. Rapists cannot justify (though they may explain) their action by pointing out that they are less favorably situated for seduction and less likely to persuade the girl (or the university) than a better-endowed or richer suitor. Yet most of the argument for violent action is simply that persuasion might not succeed—as though this justified force.

Lincoln's Misleading Description of Democracy

Attempts to make "formal" democracy, as a set of rules or procedures, more attractive by stressing the substantive results to be expected from the procedures, have long been part of the American tradition. But few American theoreticians have been willing to trade in the formal procedures for the sake of the substantive results promised by a "dictatorship of the elite"; fewer still would accept the idea that what is to be given up is not "true" freedom; and hardly any that dictatorship is, or will lead to it. Nonetheless, the substantive definition of democracy, which relies on results or promises, and the procedural one, which relies on the intrinsic worth of self-government, have often been combined and confused. In this, FDR followed a tradition which goes back at least to Abraham Lincoln.

Lincoln's ringing "government of the people, by the people, and for the people" is a characterization of democracy and of its expected effects that "shall not perish from the earth." But as a definition it is useless and misleading. "Democracy" defines a relationship between two groups, a large one, the people, and a small one, the government, such that the government derives its just powers from the people. The two cannot be identical. If democracy were literally "government *by* the people" there would be only one group, the people. Only after recognizing two separate groups—people and government—can we define their relationship and specify their mutual powers and, finally, indicate how members of one group become members of the other. Unless we acknowledge that democracy is government by the people's agents—the government—and therefore, not by the people, we cannot restrict the power of either.

Regarded as a definition, the first part of Lincoln's characterization would be self-defeating: it eliminates the distinction between the elements to be defined. But the last part of Lincoln's phrase would give us license to define as "democracy" its very opposite! If democracy is defined as "government for the people" a well-meaning and clever tyrant who governs "for the people" (that is, in their best interest) could not be regarded as a tyrant. A foolish democratic regime, unsuccessful in its enterprises, or a democratic regime which by mandate of the people (who might misconceive their interests) does not govern "for the people" would cease to be democratic according to this definition. So also would a democratic government ousted by the opposition in a free vote, for the opposition usually clamors that the government to be replaced is not "for the people." And if the opposition wins, the voters have agreed. Are we to conclude then, paradoxically, that only tyrannical governments—which cannot be ousted—are "for the people" and thus democratic? Indeed, any tyrant who merely believes that his tyranny is for the people—and what tyrant does not?—could rightly claim that it is democratic. Hitler and Stalin would become prime democrats by this criterion. For how is it to be decided whether their claim is true? They won't permit a free vote. But to say "that refusal makes them undemocratic" is to imply that the people's ability to oust governments freely and peacefully is what makes a system democratic. Whether the ousted government was run "for the people" is immaterial then. All that matters is whether the people are free to oust it.

We have no objective way of deciding what or who is "for the people." If we did there would be no need for decision by voting. We should install the government that could objectively be shown to govern "for the people." We should leave government to experts as we do engineering. What is distinctive about democracy is not that the "government is for the people," but that the people are perpetually able to decide whether they are for the government. Neither the wisdom of the people's decision, nor of their government, makes a regime democratic; the power kept by the people to make decisions on who is to govern does. The people's decisions can be misguided. Possibly a dictatorship could do better for them, at least at times. But democracy is not defined by any result. It must be defined as a process by which the citizens keep the power to elect a government as foolish or wise as they see fit and to correct their mistakes or make them worse.

The wisdom of a democratic government in the end depends on the wisdom of the people who elect it. The tragedy of democracy may be, as Santayana thought, that people "do as they wish but do not get what they want." If so, at least democracy does not allow the government to decide what the citizens want by disregarding the wishes they express or by forestalling expression. God reads our hearts' desires better than we do. But it is unlikely that governments will. And they might misread their own desires into our muted hearts. To fail in what we want by getting what we wish is part of the human tragedy. In democracy we face it and suffer the fulfillment of our own desires, however foolish.

For many this is not enough, or, perhaps, too much. In considering what may lead them to violence, we must distinguish (A) the basic conditions which generally and permanently dispose people to dissatisfaction which may culminate in political violence; (B) the specific conditions which may intensify resentment and precipitate violence; (C) the conditions which dispose specific groups to violence at particular times.

Causes of Political Violence

A. Resentment of the Human Condition: The Dream of Paradise Regained Lingers On

Chiliastic Hopes

Since time immemorial men have felt that they lost paradise and have longed for it. Ovid's description in his *Metamorphoses*[*] hardly differs from the description of prelapsarian bliss in Genesis. Christians expect to be redeemed from this vale of tears and to regain paradise upon the final judgment. This is a long time to wait for salvation, and some always were impatient. In the Middle Ages they often relied on the promise—found most explicitly in Revelation (20:4–6)—that the Messiah, upon his Second Coming, would resurrect those who had faithfully suffered and worked for him. They would get a preview of things to come, for he would rule them on earth for a thousand years, to the day of judgment, when the rest of humanity too would be resurrected. Hence those Christians who, impatient for the redemption of the divine promise, were not above hurrying salvation along, were called millenarians by readers of the Vulgate (and chiliasts by readers of the Greek gospels). Millenarians always were enthusiasts as well (from *en theos*); they thought God had revealed to them—but not to the degenerate official

[*] See p. 16.

authorities—how to prepare for the imminent Millennium and be saved. And usually they were antinomians: the return of the Messiah required that they overthrow the existing social order. People unwilling to relinquish their mundane advantages, or unconvinced of the divine authority of the millenarian prophets, were slain without hesitation. Their mission exempted millenarian leaders from the mores and moralities of ordinary times and men. The Millennium, just as does "the revolution," requires human sacrifices to become authoritative and credible. Millenarian movements thus always have been given to violence—to the use of force and to the violation of norms.

Early Christians thought salvation so imminent that theologians had a hard job pushing redemption of the promise beyond this temporal world. They succeeded with the faithful as a whole. But in times of stress, millenarian movements always sprung up to expect immediate salvation and, in preparation, to rebel against the ecclesiastic and temporal authorities who, by their sinful conduct and by their lack of faith, were believed to retard salvation. Indeed, they had been unable to avert the social calamities which fired the hope of redemption and made it urgent. Economic or military reverses can produce stress. But so can endogenous developments which lead to social conflicts or to the erosion of the value system shared by the members of society.

Paradise Lost

The expectation of salvation by a Messiah is only one of many forms utopian thinking and wishing has taken. Though it be rationalized in different ways, responding to the specific discontents and deprivations of each historical period, millenarianism rests on the most profound common aspirations and fears of mankind—on the paradise we actually lost: on a dim, and largely unconscious memory of our own prehistory.

In our religious tradition, the human predicament and the need for salvation from it both derive from Adam's Fall—the *felix culpa* about which we have always been ambivalent. In the words John Milton heard from Adam's lips:

> Full of doubt I stand
> Whether I should repent men now of sin
> By me done or occasioned, or rejoice
> Much more, that much more good
>   thereof shall spring—

We have always looked with longing to the paradise lost and with dread, doubt, yet also pride on what this loss made possible: the human career on earth—history.

How were we locked out of the Garden of Eden? Genesis tells us that by eating the fruit from the forbidden tree we became "wise"; we came "to know good and evil." Ontogeny repeats phylogeny. Every child is expelled in turn from the Garden of Eden—expelled by his years—to know "good and evil," to become human if not "wise." As we grow up, *nolente volente* we are seized with reason and, therefore, with responsibility. To translate this into psychological language more familiar today: each of us has to renounce the pure pleasure principle and his (polymorphously perverse) innocence to "eat bread in the sweat of his face," to acquire an ego, to engage in object relations, to work and extract sustenance from a harsh and niggardly nature, to make peace with reality. And each of us acquires a superego perpetuating the burden of original sin, of Oedipal guilt. We all rebel against the father and fall from his grace. The need for the sacrificial "son of man" *agnus Dei qui tollit peccata mundi** is therefore universally felt. Freud and the writers of Genesis concur: civilization (as well as its discontents) rests on our revolt against paternal rule.

* The lamb of God which bears the sins of the world.

Chiliasm Rationalized

Rationalists have always denied the endogenous and necessary nature of the Fall and of the consequent "corruption" of human nature. They have always felt that paradise can be regained cheaply—if we are but reasonable and listen to them. They do not see that to reenter Eden would be to give up the very gift of reason they wish us to use as a key: for to be in paradise is to be sinless—unaware of right and wrong.

Paradise so far remains as elusive as ever. But our longing has not diminished. And those who now would lead us into it regard it as a demonstrable possibility of human nature, a natural rather than a supernatural place. Freud is alleged to have held the key; but he failed to unlock the gate because he lacked courage and Marxist training. Herbert Marcuse and Norman O. Brown will lead us where he did not dare go.*

In its current form, Pelagian rationalism[31] goes back to the platonic Socrates, who equated happiness with virtue and virtue with knowledge, while vice was but ignorance. Aristotle modified this view by acknowledging *akrasia*—the weakness of the will, which may lead us to do what we know to be wrong. Virtue thus becomes rejection of (external) temptation. It was mainly Christianity that recognized the positive evil in us—what Freud was to call the death instinct. It is this inherent corruption, or, if you wish, the tension of human existence that rationalists are still busy denying; they depict evil as exogenous, social, and altogether correctible.

The idea that man is born and could remain good is as death-

---

* See Herbert Marcuse, *Eros and Civilization* (New York: Vintage Books, 1962) and Norman O. Brown, *Life against Death* (Middletown, Conn.: Wesleyan University Press, 1959).

31. Pelagian Heresy (p. 122).

less as the wish from which it springs. The fact that, at most, men can become better is hard to face. J. J. Rousseau's disastrous dictum "Nature has made man happy and good—society corrupts him and causes his misery" seems to be the more accepted the more observation shows it to be false, and the more the search for a worldly paradise turns out to be vain.

From the Founding Fathers to Educational Salvationism

Unlike many of their recent eulogists, most of the Founding Fathers of this country were too shrewd to believe in man's innate goodness or, at least, to rely on it. They did not "trust the people" as they are often accused of having done. Our Constitutional checks and balances represent the institutionalization of their distrust of human beings; it proved salutary.

Our checks and balances were not instituted then because, in Lord Acton's pseudoprofound phrase, "Power tends to corrupt and absolute power corrupts absolutely," but, on the contrary, because the Founding Fathers knew bad men are as likely to corrupt good institutions as bad institutions are to corrupt good men. Power merely makes corruption effective, as it does all our inclinations. That is why we must control it, why the power of any person must be restrained by that of others interested in wielding their own and restraining his. Yet power itself is only as corrupt as we are; it is not corrupting. A leopard may dream of eating people but lack the power to do so as long as he is restrained by his cage. When the cage collapses, he has the power to eat people. It is not the power—the collapsed cage, the ability to attack without restraint—that produces the appetite; power merely makes it possible to satisfy it.* Those who disregard this

* The wish to achieve or keep power (ambition) may cause us to act corruptly—but not the power itself. The situation is analogous with money, which is a form of power, and with other objects of desire.

distinction are easily beguiled by the eschatology of modern millenarianism which depicts the powerless as *ipso facto* good and contends that the institutions which restrain human corruption and cruelty cause what they restrain.

Rousseau and Acton are moderate compared with Condorcet's follower, Cabanis, who summarized the creed of the Enlightenment prophets: "*Les méchants ne sont que des mauvais raisonneurs.*" (Wicked people just reason incorrectly.) Some form of this rationalist belief is implied in our revivalist enthusiasm for education as a panacea for all the world's ills—ills which we regard as mistakes due to ignorance or, taking *akrasia* into account, as the effects of wrong conditioning also correctible by means of education. In fact, however, education is a neutral vehicle which can distribute and amplify evil as well as good. When it raises ambition beyond fulfillment, education is likely to lead to restlessness and resentment.

Education can be *defined* as an ideal process effectively leading to goodness (as seen by the proponent), as that which produces the desired results. But does it actually? If we define education as the empirical process of schooling (not, as we tend to do, as desirable and automatically successful learning) its effects are seen to depend on how the process is used and on the users. The schools at best can make actions—whether good or bad ones—more effective. And schools necessarily reflect and stress the attitudes of parents, teachers, governments and students. Moreover, student attitudes are formed by many outside factors. The school's role can neither be decisive nor independent. Finally, we do not know how to control the process of attitude formation even in the comparatively regulated scholastic environments. Or, perhaps, we refrain from controlling it because we disagree on what attitudes we want formed. One must conclude that the hope of salvation through schooling is misplaced. Presecularized chiliasm, which expected salvation from grace, seems more reasonable. No one can show what grace cannot do.

Chiliastic Elitism

Political utopians never explain how a society which corrupts all its members, however naturally good they be, can find people to reform it. Religious salvationists, of course, have "grace" to explain their mission. Secular salvationists cannot offer this explanation. They have none. More than intellectual untidiness is involved. Political millenarians usually are reluctant to explain that they form an elite which alone has transcended the corruption of the rest of us. They seldom openly advocate their own dictatorship. Marcuse's candor is commendable but exceptional. Yet such a dictatorship is implied by all those ready to use violence to overthrow the imperfect institutions of formal democracy.

From Rousseau to Marx and to "Surplus Repression"

Rousseau's most influential, though unacknowledged heir, Karl Marx, explained specifically how we are corrupted and made miserable by capitalist institutions. Marx completed the secularization of utopian thinking by explaining the corrupting capitalist system as historically unavoidable yet *ipso facto* temporary. He was contemptuous of old-fashioned (pre- or non-Marxist) utopians who did not extrapolate their visions of the future from "history." Because he did, he regarded himself as the founder of *scientific* socialism. Marx also scorned "old-fashioned" utopians because they offered explicitly moral justifications for their schemes, whereas he predicted, on "scientific" grounds, what his, or rather history's, scheme was, and how it would come into being. In the post-Hegelian manner, the future was regarded as *eo ipso* morally right: morality is either identical with historical developments or irrelevant. Thus, after having corrupted them, history (which takes the place of a relentless Manichean God) will save the faithful—subject to the usual millenarian conditions: they must make sacrifices but, above all, they must believe. Those who reject the revelation of history's prophet and his marching orders are not only damned but also doomed; and the faithful, executing history's orders, will help that doom along.

This is not the occasion for a critique of Marx's often quite instructive but mostly circular reasoning, or of his propositions which restate, disguised as empirical demonstrations of the unavoidable developments of capitalism, what is already implied in his evaluative definitions. For example, the value of output exceeds that of input. The excess is—by definition—created exclusively by workers; they are exploited, therefore, inasmuch as this excess ("surplus value") does not go to them. Of course, one may as well define capital as the exclusive source of excess (surplus) value and regard its owners as exploited if they do not get all of it. It all depends on what one quite arbitrarily defines as the source of the excess ("surplus"); its quantity depends as well on what is defined as the "value" of the ingredients of production. Obvious? Not if one elaborates it in three volumes nor if one has uncritically accepted the problem as posed by the classical economists.*

If it is difficult to draw specific inferences (other than moral ones) from Marx's "surplus value," Marcuse's analogous psychological concept of "surplus repression" (repression functionally needed under capitalism—but not in a better system) adds nothing to the truism that in some indirect way culture affects individual character—and, therewith, what one accepts, rejects, or represses. Marcuse nowhere explains why capitalism more than socialism requires repression of, say, homosexual or sadistic inclinations, or of affectionate feelings. He simply declares "bad" repression "surplus" and attributes it to capitalism. The Marxian

* Paul Samuelson's "Understanding the Marxist Notion of Exploitation," *The Journal of Economic Literature* (June 1971) is perhaps the most generous and final critique.

economic surplus, at least, exists, however arbitrary Marx was in imputing it to workers. But Marcuse's psychological "surplus repression" is a purely moral category miraculously generated by capitalism and disappearing with it.

Actually the problem of repression is not one of excessive amounts ("surplus") but of what is repressed, how and with what effects. That selection is not specifically determined by any economic system, although (noneconomic) cultural factors may affect it. Wherefore the selection by Russian or Chinese socialism resembles that of Victorian capitalism more than the selection by American capitalism does. Thus, Chinese and Russian socialists may repress sexual spontaneity and diversity more than American capitalists. Individuality too is certainly more repressed in socialist systems. On the other hand, capitalism cultivates communal feelings less. How Marcuse's concept of capitalist "surplus repression" helps understand all this—or for that matter anything else—is hard to see.

That much to suggest why people believe that paradise was lost through oppression and exploitation, economic and psychological, and can be regained by violence used to change the political and economic system. The belief is not rational. But it is motivated so strongly that ever new rationalizations are accepted even by those who pride themselves on their own rationality and on their understanding of history.

B. Conditions That Precipitate Violence

Poverty

Material matters have improved for most Americans and have improved most for those least favored in the past. Thus, by the definition used by the Bureau of Labor Statistics (adjusted for

changes in the purchasing power of money), 20 percent of all
families were "poor" in 1962, while in 1967 less than 11 percent
were: 8.4 percent of white families and 30.7 percent of non-
whites. A decade earlier more than 15 percent of the white and
more than half of the nonwhite families were "poor." This decrease of the size of the "poor" group is a long-standing trend, as
is the decrease of their distance from "average" income. That the
effective legal rights of all religious and racial groups are more
equal—and greater—now than they were fifty years ago is hardly
a secret. Why then riots and threats of violence by self-appointed
spokesmen for the disadvantaged?

Riots as Punishments

Many people feel that riots have come as a punishment for our
sins and, therefore, are best avoided by repentance and repair.*
Rioters and would-be rioters have capitalized on this explanation.
They have been successful with some churches and politicians;
which, by allowing themselves to be blackmailed, merely en-
couraged further riots.

Possibly we deserve every punishment we get and more. But
sin and punishment must not be confused with cause and effect.
Whatever morally deserves punishment is not *ipso facto* the
cause of punishment, however much the punishment is felt to be
deserved. A theory of crime and punishment dictated by the
guilty consciences of those who hold it is not a reliable guide for
investigating and predicting cause and effect—conscience is a
guide only to normative matters.

The causes of which the riots were effects were not our sins,
however blameworthy, but our virtues, however praiseworthy.
In the secularized para-Marxist version of the crime (sin) and

* E.g., the Report of President Johnson's National Advisory Commission
on Civil Disorders, 1968 (Kerner Commission).

punishment theory, riots occur because white society is rich and allows, or causes, Negroes to be poor in its midst. More mundane means of investigation suggest that the contrast between rich and poor (including blacks) was greater in the past, is greater in most European countries (let alone Asiatic and African ones) and in America is greatest where there were least riots—and that the riots no more were caused by our sins than the epidemics of bubonic plague, or the sack of Rome, were caused by the unquestioned sinfulness of the population. On the contrary, the riots were caused by our attempts to repent, to repair the harm done, and above all, by suggestions or promises implying that we will and can do so instantly. Regardless of action taken, such promises were bound to disappoint. They led to resentment and, finally, violence. Frustration is caused by the difference between what one expects, or feels oneself entitled to, and what one actually gets. It often leads to aggression, which may become violent if frustration is felt acutely, if violence seems justifiable, and if those who use it can hope that it will not be punished. Even if ineffective instrumentally, violence may be rewarding expressively. The Kennedy and Johnson administrations created the conditions required to precipitate violence—although the grievances expressed go back to the post-Civil War era.

De Tocqueville on Riots

Riots usually occur not despite, but because of rapid improvements. Improvements, at least in the initial stages tend to intensify dissatisfactions and mobilize preexisting resentments. The point was made well by Alexis de Tocqueville:

> It is natural that the love of equality should constantly increase together with equality itself, and that it should grow by what it feeds on. . . . When a people which has put up with an oppressive rule over a long period without protest suddenly finds the govern-

ment relaxing its pressure, it takes up arms against it. . . . Experience teaches us that, generally speaking, the most perilous moment for a bad government is one when it seeks to mend its ways. . . . The mere fact that certain abuses have been remedied draws attention to the others and they now appear more galling; people may suffer less, but their sensibility is exacerbated.

Modern empirical research states these matters less succinctly and elegantly but confirms them amply. The inevitable is tolerated, the inadequate is not. Improvement as a process leads to more dissatisfaction than static misery, for aspiration fueled by the process of improvement pulls ahead of any possible fulfillment.

The Catalinarian promises of President Kennedy and the naive attempts of President Johnson to implement them were among major causes of our riots. Both increased the expectations of the blacks beyond any possibility of fulfillment and, perhaps, beyond intention. Both Presidents also suggested that the blacks were "deprived" of what they were entitled to. So did a number of federally financed agencies engaged in the "war against poverty." The feeling thus generated, or intensified, may have helped rationalize violence. Nonetheless, the very politicians and academicians who helped provoke the outbreak were surprised by it. Not to realize this is to underestimate their generosity and their naïvete. Both are well (if unwittingly) documented by the Kerner Commission report.

The subsequent failure to reassert the Kennedy-Johnson promises, the "benign neglect," of rhetoric, and the continued actual progress toward equalization of rights and conditions are the cause of relative tranquility since. The belief that authorities will be more resolute than before in repressing violence forcefully may well have contributed to tranquility. But what led middle-class students to take over from poor blacks?

C. What Made Some Students Violent?

Educational Inflation

More than 42 percent of college-age youths now attend college, while only 25 percent of the age group have the I.Q. (over 110) required to benefit from college education. To be sure, many of these students are still sheltered in community and junior colleges. But this defense of academic standards, porous to begin with, is not likely to last. "Education" has taken the place formerly occupied by religion in the sentiments of many Americans. It is felt to be good for everybody—by definition. More and more money and people are pumped into higher education without much thought being given to the abilities of the participants and to the qualities and, above all, the actual effects of the education given.

Until its inflation reduces college education to high school levels—a process which has only begun—more and more students will find college irrelevant to them. This is unavoidable, unless faculties realize that these students are irrelevant to the college. Yet faculties are unlikely to do so, since they are in the same boat with the students: far more people teach and do research than are competent to do either. Faculties as well as student bodies expand with available money, and faster by far than available talent. Under these circumstances restless students, led by restless professors, will abound for some time to come. The restlessness can be held in bounds—this side of violence—only by the assertion of the authority to expel disruptive students. Without this assertion students will continue to be restless at least as long as "confrontation" is more "relevant"—i.e., status conferring—than study. For those incapable of benefiting from study this may be permanently so. But others are as restless; indeed, originally many "confrontations" were led by able students who preferred them to the studies they were intellectually able—but emotionally unwilling—to pursue. What directed their ambition from academic careers to confrontations?

Schopenhauer on Sources of Unhappiness

In the nineteenth century, Arthur Schopenhauer pointed to two major sources of human unhappiness: deprivation, which frustrates the poor, and surfeit, which causes the boredom of the rich. The poor are stimulated, or at least kept busy, but unsatisfied. It is their dissatisfaction which keeps them occupied. The rich are materially satisfied but unstimulated. The poor wish for money and leisure to free them from deprivation; the rich for challenge and meaningful activity to free them from boredom. When the two wishes coalesce, when the rich seek their challenge in leading the poor into opposing the conditions alleged to make them poor, the setting for violence exists.

Frustration of the Affluent Young

In the past the rich were few, and many were still engaged in the activities which tradition and education, if not material need, had made meaningful to them. Now the poor are few—11 percent, rather than half of the population as in the 1920s—wherefore they are isolated and more resentful than ever. Life has passed them by; they have been left behind and feel "underprivileged."

The many newly affluent people keep busy but find no satisfying ways to engage time, which hangs heavy on their hands. Unprepared for leisure, they can no longer kill time altogether by making money: the challenge and the moral significance that gave meaning to this activity have diminished too much. Money has lost its authority, though not its power. Time stays alive to bore them. It bores their children even more. They never had to work out of necessity and, in many cases, they have found no effort worth their while. The parents and schools who should have led them to meaningful efforts, to the discipline of work, to respect for achievement, have failed them. These children are desperate for the challenge of meaningful activity or, in its absence, at least for distraction from the boredom that makes time such a heavy burden to bear. They are as sullen and resentful as the poor were thought to be in the past.

Dedication to Ward off Tedium

Sex and drugs serve to distract, as does the conspicuous consumption of the self, engaged in by so many. But these do not yield the transcendent challenge and the sense of dedication ultimately required to ward off tedium. As Ortega y Gasset foresaw: "an 'unengaged' existence is a worse negation of life than death itself. . . . Before long there will be heard throughout the planet a formidable cry, like the howling of innumerable dogs to the stars asking . . . to impose an occupation, a duty."* We are surfeited with leisure, liberty, affluence and therewith boredom. The direct pursuit of pleasure turns out to be an onerous task for most of the young, and, in the end, unrewarding.

Yet some students are unable to pursue anything else. Others fervently insist that everybody follow their ideals, which usually are generous and gentle, and so gushily formulated as to be unobjectionable: peace, equality, freedom, creativity, love, sincerity, everybody doing his own thing (even nothing if he can't find anything to engage him). There is little understanding of the obstacles to the realization of such ideals, of their mutual inconsistency, of their clash with the requirements of any social order, of their unspecificity and ambiguity, which causes them to

* *The Revolt of the Masses* (New York: Mentor, 1951), p. 99.

be beside the point, quite insufficient to meet the problems, or devise the compromises which settle the conflicts of any feasible society. The only obstacles these "radicals" can see are the demons Marx secularized: oppressive capitalists, uptight racists, and overly repressed middle classes. More love and more revolution will remedy all that.

Doing Your Thing

Some "radicals" do not even wish to understand that to do nothing is to live at someone else's expense, off his labor; and that to demand as much as a right is to demand the right to exploit others. They meet objections with fantasies produced by journalism and science fiction: "scarcity" and, therewith, work could be abolished any day; or with the assertion of a "right" to be paid for a contribution not valued by others, a "right" to be employed to produce something not demanded or to work at a job not available. They refuse to realize that this "right" would be a right to exploit others by compelling them to give what they value—their work or its fruits—for something without value to them.

Similarly, many youthful radicals shrilly proclaim the desirability of peace, love, and so on, but do not see that no one denies it— that there is disagreement only on how to achieve and preserve peace, love, and so on. It is simpler to picture opponents (the establishment) as hateful warmongers. Attempts to confront the actual intellectual issues are as rare as attempts to confront the dean are frequent.

Rates of Change and Authority

Our rate of technological and social change is so high (and continuously accelerating) that the authority of tradition—authority is never less than a tradition—and of those bearing and transmitting it was bound to be greatly impaired. And, therewith, the authority of all established social institutions and values, particularly of universities: the institutions charged with transmission of knowledge, tradition, experience and learning and with preparing the young for established social roles. Our life has become too discontinuous—as has our culture—to grant authority to anything but present power. Whence violence becomes acceptable.

Causes of Action

Actions occur only when the desire prompting them exceeds the desire to avoid the expected cost. That cost may be inherent (the effort to be made), economic (demanded by others to compensate for their effort), legal (penalties imposed by society to deter law violations), or moral (pangs of one's own conscience produced by violation of internalized rules). There are two ways of preventing actions then: by reducing the desire for them, or by raising the expected cost of fulfilling the desire. In universities neither was done.[32]

Authority and Authoritarianism

One frequent reason for not increasing the cost of violence was confusion of authority and authoritarianism. Authoritarianism involves illegitimate authority, or its illegitimate use, or the assertion of authority beyond its jurisdiction, or in circumstances in which it is not needed or, finally, the idea that authority must be "total." Authority was confused with authoritarianism and discredited by the emergence and the careers of Stalin, Hitler and Mussolini.* It takes imagination to confuse an assertion of

32. Leniency (p. 123).

* It is seldom understood that the last two were reactions to the weakening of authority—yet Lincoln already warned that "people become tired of

legitimate democratic authority with their dictatorships. Faculties showed no lack of imagination.

Authority, Consent and Consensus

Many officials vaguely feel that since authority in a democracy must rest on consent, each specific act of authority must be ratified by a consensus. Yet, although the authority of laws, courts, or universities rests on consent, particular judgments, procedures, rules, or enforcements do not. Otherwise law and authority are replaced by consensus.

However irrational, the feeling that they could not act against what appeared as consensus was powerful enough among university officials to make them hesitate. The craving for popularity dominant among officeholders, who all to often have little else to measure their own value by, makes the assertion of authority against nonconsenting groups psychologically hard—unless these groups first have been defined as being beyond the pale. Students clearly are not. On the contrary, they are treated as though a political constituency which must be catered to to obtain reelection or a group of consumers that must be induced to buy. Indeed, the youth worship bordering on pedophilia, which has long been a part of our social life, makes it very hard for an American to believe that the younger generation can be wrong in any conflict between generations.

Because students seemed disaffected, faculties and administrations felt that they must have been guilty of some crime—which radical students hastened to define as possession of authority. They succeeded in making professors and administrators search their souls instead of asserting the authority of learning

---

and disgusted with a government that offers them no protection. . . ." ("The Perpetuation of Our Political Institutions") 1838.

vested in them. Where did we go wrong, they asked; and each came up with a different answer.

A Right to Speak—an Obligation to Listen?

Some told themselves that limited violence (an academic concept if there ever was one) is a legitimate method to get the university (or the government, or the majority) to listen and that, therefore, such violence is covered by the constitutional protection of free speech. Yet free speech does not cover coercion, violence, or even trespass. And, although the constitution grants a right to free speech, it does not impose a duty to listen; certainly there is no obligation whatever to do what those who are permitted to speak freely want. Such an obligation would restrict and coerce those listeners (or nonlisteners) who are opposed to the demands of the speakers. The right to persuade does not imply an obligation to be persuaded; nor is lack of success proof that those who failed were not free to try, and are, therefore, entitled to violence.

The Cost of Violence

When authority is not exercised to increase the cost of violence, violence is not likely to decrease. Less than 3 percent of all crimes committed are punished now, usually mildly and after tremendous delays. The uncertainty and the delay rob punishment of its deterrent effect. Crime and violence will not be deterred until the actual cost to those engaged in both—punishment —is increased and, above all, made more swift and certain. Violence will increase as long as the price of gratifying the desire for it does not. It is one of the few prices that has actually been reduced in recent history, inflation notwithstanding. Our educational institutions are likely to continue to foster violence indirectly by their refusal to expel students engaged in it. Schools thereby teach students that they can engage in violence with impunity—one lesson they have been quick to learn.

The Future

The remarkable ineptitude of the leaders of our society in all this is certainly unpleasant to contemplate. Yet it does not demonstrate that our democratic institutions are in danger of being overthrown by violence. If their defenders are not endowed with much wisdom and firmness, their enemies are too few, too marginal and too silly. Above all, they lack the support of any major segment of society. It is not that the cost of the attempt is too high—we have made it rather low—but that most Americans do not support violence because they are not sufficiently dissatisfied. Although few see the achievements of our system clearly, most people feel them sufficiently to oppose a violent change. Yet, if we continue unlimited tolerance of the violent minority, it may succeed in producing a revolution—or a reaction which will reduce the limits of tolerance beyond necessity. Neither prospect is pleasant to contemplate.

NOTES TO CIVIL DISOBEDIENCE

1. Disobedience by military personnel to military authority is usually called insubordination or, when violent and concerted, mutiny, regardless of whether moral principles play a role. (Insubordination refers to disobedience to superiors within any organization.)
2. Abe Fortas' view which requires that "the law being violated, itself, [be] the focus, or target of, the protest" (*Concerning Dissent and Civil Disobedience* [New York: 1968], p. 63) would exclude most acts usually and properly defined as civil disobedience.
3. To challenge the validity of a putative law by disobeying it, and to have it declared invalid, is actually to show that one did not disobey a valid law, but successfully challenged an authority which thought otherwise. Hence, literally, to regard the successful challenge as civil disobedience is to confuse lawful resistance to unlawful commands of authority with unlawful resistance to lawful commands. And, contrary to what is widely believed, successful defense does not vindicate civil disobedience, any more than successful defense of a person charged with murder vindicates murder. The defense is successful only by showing that the accused did not disobey (or was not shown to have disobeyed) a (valid) law. Its success,

therefore, cannot vindicate his having done so. But these legal or logical distinctions have little bearing on the essentially moral problem.

4. Howard Zinn, in *Disobedience and Disorder* (New York: Vintage, 1968), argues that those engaged in civil disobedience have no reason to submit to punishment inflicted by laws which they reject. He ignores, rather than refutes, the reason Socrates gave for doing so: the general obligation of the citizen to obey the laws, even though that obligation must sometimes yield to a higher one. The higher obligation would force Socrates to disobey laws directly inconsistent with it, but not legal procedures which he did not repudiate, and not, therefore, the verdict validly produced through them, however unjust he thought it to be. Zinn's proposal also would (as he half acknowledges) leave civil disobedience shorn of its symbolic and persuasive character—it would make invisible the distinction between a person who resists the draft on moral grounds and one who dodges it for nonmoral reasons. Both would flee. Zinn's counsel would be consistent with preparing revolution however, though not necessarily wise: revolution, unlike civil disobedience, opposes the whole system rather than specific laws and may fight it by whatever means are found effective.

5. "Moral duty" is here used as synonym for (moral) "obligation" which is binding, not by external force nor by threat of external punishment, but because the person obligated *feels* bound without (external) coercion. He could, but feels he ought not to, act otherwise. He chooses to act according to his obligation; and even if he does not, he may acknowledge it by regarding his act as immoral, or feeling a conflict about it.

Much of people's behavior must be explained by their sense of obligation. It is acquired as part of the socialization process, and, therefore, differs as far as the objects of obligation are concerned, from society to society. But the sense of obligation exists in all societies. Examples of the sense of obligation in our society may include unrequited kindness, sacrifice, risk-taking for the sake of others, performing duties or fulfilling promises when one could do otherwise to one's (material) advantage, loyalties, and, not least, doing things for the sake of moral principle.

Discussion of the sense of obligation—how it is acquired, strengthened, weakened, attached to objects or ideas—is part of psychology. Discussion of obligation *per se*—how it is defined, justified, what it entails, where it lies, how an obligation fits with other obligations—is part of moral and political philosophy; it is what engages us here.

6. Yet, civil disobedience attempts to persuade by acts, however symbolic; and these acts are not protected by the First Amendment freedom of speech because they involve more than communication: one thing is to say something should (or should not) be done; it is quite another thing to do (or not to do) it, even if only paradigmatically. However, if the acts themselves are *altogether* symbolic, if they deal exclusively with symbols, such as the flag, we may have a conflict of rights: the right of society to protect the symbols it lives by and the right of individuals to freely express themselves by using symbols must be balanced against each other.

7. In later years Gandhi repudiated this instrumental use of himself. While continuing to approve of self-imposed suffering and of using such suffering for persuasion, he repudiated his use of the threat of self-destruction as a means of pressure to impose his wishes on others. He knew, of course, that they were threatened not only by losing him, but also by the possible popular reaction—probably violent—to the loss. "Truth force," as he redefined it, was to be entirely persuasive, eschewing pressure and coercion and threats even of self-destruction.

8. Jesus, in this conception, becomes a victim not of avoidable injustice, but of unavoidable social need stemming from the

fall of man, which calls for law and order and for its victims (innocent as well as guilty). Redemption from law and order, salvation, requires a regained state of innocence where neither laws nor victims are needed. Such salvation is possible because of His sacrifice—after history ends.

9. So did all later utopians up (or down) to Herbert Marcuse and Norman O. Brown. E.g., J. J. Rousseau: "Nature has made man happy and good—society corrupts him and causes his misery." In contrast, the Christian religion has insisted on the consequences of Adam's fall. In a different conceptual framework, so does nonutopian science. Yet modern utopians differ from ancient ones by relying on "science" rather than religion, although actual science contradicts the empirical (psychological, economic, or social) propositions on which the utopian fantasy so largely rests.

10. To deprive the minority of these liberties, be it by majority vote or by inducing even a unanimous group to renounce them, is to give up democracy. See Sidney Hook, *The Paradoxes of Freedom* (Berkeley, Calif.: University of California Press, 1962), Part 3 *passim.*

11. There is an unresolved problem in democratic theory here. If an issue can be treated as local, or divisible, it can be decided differently by separate groups; but, despite material divisibility, an issue may be conceived so that one uniformly applied decision must be made by an overall majority. Possibly, a local, a regional, or an overall majority might each decide differently. Thus, there may be a conflict of majorities among each other, of majorities in different groups, instead of one between majority and minority in the same group.

There are no grounds for holding imposition of the wishes of the overall majority on the local majority to be in principle more democratic than allowing separate (democratic) decisions in each separate group. Hence it would be beside the point in such a case to speak of minority or majority imposition. The definition of voting units and of their jurisdictions, the actual issue here, depends on one's view of the divisibility of the issue, and on one's ideas about centralization, or decentralization, in decision making. Definitions of voting units do not follow set rules; they are shaped by historical factors as much as by material ones. (Among recent conflicts on this issue are: Nigeria-Biafra, France-Algeria, Portugal-Mozambique, U.S.-local school boards, states, and communities.)

Another issue arises largely from confusion. While democrats regard democracy as appropriate to make decisions in political units, however delimited, they do not necessarily favor this form of governance for nonpolitical organizations or functions such as jails, business firms, ships, armies, hospitals, or universities. The "democratic" requirement (interpreted as decision making by majorities and elective office holding) may defeat the purpose of the organization (e.g., education, imprisonment, fighting) or be inconsistent with the different functions and competences of the persons involved, or, finally, with their different shares of investment in the organization.

Democratic decision making is possible, and desirable (in some respects) even in nonpolitical organizations when there are no significant differences in function, competence, permanence of membership, investment, and so on. Where there are such differences, the purpose of the organization might be defeated by "democratic" voting. Who would invest in a firm in which noninvestors—e.g., employees—determine wages and policies by majority vote? How could students determine the scholarly competence of professors whose field they have not studied, and who, by definition, are more competent than students to determine scholarly competence? How can patients or nurses determine how operations are to be carried out or by whom? or how high the budget for the pathology department ought to be?

On the issue: who should govern the country? we are probably all equally competent (or incompetent). At least I can see no way of deciding who is more or less competent: evaluations and standards of evaluation of desirable policies and candidates differ irresolvably. It cannot be shown that the more intelligent or educated vote or govern better than others. Yet ultimately, we are all affected by the government regardless of whether we want to be; there is nothing we can do about it except vote for what we prefer. However, we can fairly easily avoid specific universities, hospitals, and business firms (and even prison), if we do not like the way they are run or the services they offer. The government affects everyone, while most other institutions effect only some people, who are usually quasi-volunteers and have other choices. But we rarely have the choice of being either French or American citizens. We should all have a vote about the government which unavoidably affects us. But scholars should decide on universities, investors on corporations, physicians on hospitals. Students, consumers, employees, and patients can usually switch to other universities, firms, or even hospitals if they are dissatisfied. They have considerable indirect influence.

12. Led by Kenneth Arrow (*Social Choice and Individual Values* [New York: Wiley, 1963]), mathematically inclined scholars have shown that majority votes can produce decisions which defeat the actual order of preferences of both the majority and the minority; the outcome may be contrary to the wishes of all, then, and inconsistent as well with other decisions. These arguments are correct (and were anticipated, in part, by the Marquis de Condorcet in 1785). When votes are taken among representatives of the voters, decisions are even less likely to reflect majority wishes precisely. Moreover, what the majority wills often differs from what it wants—from what it would desire if possessed of all relevant information and not influenced by anything irrelevant to the issue.

Finally, "special interest groups," because they organize to focus on particular issues (and representatives), often exercise influence far beyond their numbers and lead to decisions contrary to majority wishes. It follows that democracy often does not lead to consistent and rational decisions or express majority preferences perfectly and completely.

Certainly, thought should be given to making decisions more rational and responsive to the wants of the majority. Yet Arrow's argument is irrelevant to any discussion of the *relative* merits of democracy. The preferability of the democratic system to others could be reduced, or removed, only if it were shown that other government systems suffer less, or not at all, from the defects affecting democracy. It is obvious, however, that owing to the right of the majority to govern, and of the minority to oppose, democracy (1) is more likely to reflect the wishes of both in the long run than systems without these rights; (2) leaves both more free to form and express wishes and to try to achieve majority support; (3) is less likely than other systems, in the long run, to produce a government (or a totality of policies) much worse than desired by the citizens.

Nondemocratic systems usually do not claim to represent majority wishes; or, if they do, they do not allow the majority to freely confirm or disconfirm the claim, which thus becomes untestable. Therefore, the unavoidable qualifications of that claim, noted above, affect only the democratic system which makes it. It does not follow that nondemocratic systems achieve any better than democratic systems what they do not even claim to achieve. They do not. Indeed, crosscurrents of power or influence can cause an order of preferences to become inconsistent, or irrational, just as easily as voting procedures can. And a result which defeats the wishes and wants of most is more likely than in a democracy.

A perfect dictator can be conceived to be more rational

and more responsive to majority wishes than an imperfect democratic government. But history suggests that this possibility rarely becomes actuality. It is fairly easy to see why most dictators are worse than most elected governments. By definition, they are independent of majority consent but do need the support of some (minority) groups: even to govern by force means to depend on enforcers. But these groups may well act to thwart majority wishes, and, indeed, all but their own. Democracy, however imperfectly, permits both the majority, and, in the end, the minority too, more institutionalized influence on government and policy than any other system. Thus it guarantees more political freedom and more responsive, and no more irrational, government than any other system.

Nor do the imperfections of democracy argue against all government (i.e., in favor of anarchy). They are not relevant to the propositions on which arguments for the abolition of all government must rest. (For a different view see R. P. Wolff, *In Defense of Anarchism.*) Democratic defects cannot significantly strengthen the merits of the view that all government reduces, or eliminates, the autonomy of individuals; above all, they do not show that social life without government authority would be preferable, or even possible.

Hence, the difficulties and imperfections inherent or permitted in majoritarian voting systems, whatever intrademocratic bearing they have are quite irrelevant to a comparison of the democratic system of government with nondemocratic systems, or with no government.

13. If "moral rule" is defined as "rule binding on all," then to leave decisions to individual consciences is to relinquish moral rules. Nor could "leave it to the individual conscience" itself be justified as a moral (universal) rule, since to do so would not leave "leave it . . ." to the individual conscience. The individual conscience, being a principle of nonuniver-

sality, cannot consistently claim universality for itself or for any universal principle based on it.

14. Divine authority is, of course, binding only on the faithful. Reason, philosophers tell us, can explore the consistency and the consequences of moral principles, but it cannot by itself, establish them. And the ancient standard of "natural law" is difficult to reconcile with modern views of nature (quite apart from the different interpretations of "natural law"). That standard implied that "nature," following a path divinely traced or fulfilling an inherent, or divine, purpose would indicate to us a range of permissible and of obligatory actions. This range would be recognized by the "reason" granted to us for the purpose. The range, then, should be articulated and delimited by positive law. It would be validated or invalidated according to the faithfulness with which it applied, extended, or articulated the natural law recognized by reason.

Unfortunately, the objections to any view of "nature" as legislator seem incontrovertible. Nature opens a range of possibilities which can (and have) become actualities with varying degrees of frequency in various places and at various times. (Those possibilities which can be imagined but not actualized need not concern us: it would be pointless to legislate about them.) Natural possibilities are restricted by each society in some distinctive way (in all societies that survive, of course, so as to permit survival. But there are nearly—though not quite—infinite ways of surviving). The question is: utilization of which natural possibilities should be permitted by social authority, which should become obligatory, and which should be prohibited. This "nature" does not tell to "reason" or "science." Nature says nothing about which possibilities (including even survival) *ought* to be used, made obligatory, or excluded (and punished if used) by positive law. Nothing is "contrary to nature" if it can be done; for, if so, *nature* permits it and leaves to *our* (social or individual) decision whether to do, or permit, what nature makes possible.

The "natural law" revealed by science prescribes nothing then; it merely describes the regularities found in nature. We may derive from such natural law what effects to expect from our actions. And if we disapprove of some actions (or effects) we may prohibit them. But our disapproval and our prohibition are ours, not nature's. Moral distinctions can be made *about* nature, but they are not made, or inspired, or revealed, by nature. Above all, specific norms, rules, or principles, even if they were determined by natural human propensities—which is questionable, unless one makes it so by definition—cannot be justified by any appeal to nature, but only to our own sense of moral discrimination.

Nature has not eaten "of the tree of knowledge of good and evil." We have. The responsibility for moral rules is ours. We can make rules about nature, restricting our utilization of what it makes available. But nature does not make any rules telling us whether and how to use the possibilities it offers. To paraphrase Sidney Hook: nature does not tell whether it is more "natural" for an egg to become a chicken or an egg sandwich. Nor, whether it is "natural" to be violent or pacific, incestuous or exogamous (or neither), loving or hostile, social or antisocial. Childbirth, abortion, infanticide, conception and contraception all are natural possibilities to be morally evaluated by us—not by nature. We can reason about moral principles or derive them from revelation, but not from a study of nature which at most could help indicate the range of possibilties and effects—the question, not the answer; for what we want to know is *which* to utilize.

Some modern anthropologists and psychologists—e.g., Abraham Maslow, Erich Fromm, *et al.*—have revived natural law as "human needs" or "human nature" revealed not by "reason," but by factual (psychological or anthropological) study. They do not tell how they derive from observed behavior and its effects on mental health and happiness any rule on desirable behavior. After all, neither health nor happiness nor fulfillment of "needs"—a more impressive word for desires—can be demonstrated to be the highest goals in life. (Both Christians and the ancients have often felt it necessary to sacrifice these goals for something higher, or more important to them.) Further, one's health or happiness may derive from one's achieving the goals of his society, from gratifying the "needs" created by it; hence, these goals cannot be determined by what makes members healthy or happy, since it is achieving them—whatever they are—that does. Thus, morality as a response to "human needs" or "human nature" is no more helpful than as a response to "natural law."

Mutatis mutandis, what has been said about "natural law" applies to "natural" or "human rights," rights possessed *ab ovo, qua* human. (The more sophisticated statements in modern literature, however, demand a less summary argument than is possible on this occasion.)

15. The widespread optimistic faith that a benevolent deity has spared us all irresolvable conflicts—that, appearances to the contrary, all are effects of human misunderstanding or ignorance—although inspiring, is not supported by evidence.

16. This is not to say that conflicts can, or even should *always* be avoided. But unless the expected result is sufficiently beneficial to warrant the cost, and, unless that cost is required by the beneficial result, it is hard to justify conflict.

17. Although pointing in the right direction, this formulation may appear more helpful than it actually is. It does not tell how to compare "the totality of effects" of the two situations. The "totalities" may not be commensurable. One situation may produce cultural, the other social advantages; the first situation may increase the happiness of one group, the second

that of another; one situation may satisfy one moral criterion, the second another. We would have to assign specific weights to each of the advantages and disadvantages to calculate "the totality of expected effects" and to make a decision. As it is, we must be content with a reasoned preference.

18. Occasionally, defiance of law brings about change faster than more cumbersome lawful means. Theft, fraud, or even murder occasionally have desirable effects, too, but they hardly justify the means used to remove a wicked person or correct an unjust action. So with wicked laws or practices. Illegal means seldom can be justified unless the overthrow of the legal order can be: disobedience to law, and thus derogation, and, ultimately, abrogation of the legal order cannot be justified merely because effective, or because the direct effects are desirable in a particular instance: the indirect effects endanger everybody by endangering the legal order; they are desirable only if the legal order is not.

Civil disobedience is seldom justified to persuade, then, and even less often to coerce: not unless replacement of a popularly elected with a self-selected government is justified. Lincoln's: "there is no grievance that is a fit object of redress by mob law" ("The Perpetuation of Our Political Institutions") is but a slight exaggeration. One can conceive of such grievances. But mob law—whether imposed violently or nonviolently—is unneeded if it is possible to address the majority about redress; and dangerous if the majority is unwilling to act, for coercing it by "mob law" will seldom redress anything without bringing about worse evils.

19. It is hard to justify the conviction of Japanese leaders or the Nuremberg charge for "crimes against peace." These convictions certainly have not been regarded as precedents by any nation since, even though there were many relevant occasions, from Korea to the Middle East, to apply the precedent if Nuremberg were regarded as one.

20. To demand a right, then, is to insist on the duty of others, and, therefore, to acknowledge that one has (similar) duties toward them. To demand that one's right be enforced is to accept rights and duties of an enforcing authority. It is only by assuming that people will *spontaneously* agree on, and grant, mutual rights or fulfill mutual duties, without need for authoritative decision, or enforcement, that anarchists can deny the need for authority. Conversely, any denial of the need for authoritative decision (and enforcement) must overcome all the problems of the anarchist position. (See pp. 15–18.)

21. Dworkin does not explain why "a way he finds effective" legitimizes a citizen's act of protest. I cannot see wherein the act becomes more legitimate by being, or being thought, more effective. The question is not: is the act "effective," but is it within the law; the more effective "way" may be less legal than a less effective one, e.g., a speech.

NOTES TO POLITICAL VIOLENCE

22. The recent decline of authority stems as much from the reluctance of officials to exercise and enforce it as from refusals to accept it. In the U.S., particularly in academic institutions, the bearers of authority tend to confuse it with influence. And they often treat force as inconsistent with, rather than complementary to authority. Actually, violence can serve to preserve as well as to oppose authority. When it is used to oppose authority, violence becomes indispensable to reestablish authority.

23. Influence and power usually form a penumbra around any authority, as does violence; they are no more identical to it than violence is. Thus, ecclesiastical influence differs from *Roma locuta* (ecclesiastical authority), which, in turn, differs from secular power of enforcement.

24. This is not to reject the rather chimeric idea of *jus ad bellum* (the right to warfare) and the more concrete one of *jus in bello* (the laws of warfare) but merely to exclude them from this discussion.

   "Civil war" (groups of nearly equal strength organized to violently contend for political authority within what, at least at one point, was the same country) is neglected, for reasons of space, even though it may be considered a form of domestic violence; so is revolution (widespread violent uprisings to replace those in power and to challenge some basic principle of government), although, of course, the analysis of violence has some bearing on both. Nonpolitical violence is dealt with only indirectly to allow concentration on political violence.

25. Dostoyevsky's Grand Inquisitor argued that leave to pursue happiness is counterproductive. I believe that pursuit often is, and that leave to pursue, therefore, may be. Excessive individual freedom becomes intolerable if, by destroying community, tradition, and shared values, it collapses life into frenzy, futility and boredom. Yet too little individual freedom is stifling.

26. The original formulation listed "Freedom from Want" and did not specify "Freedom from Disease." "Freedom from Want" was interpreted as either general absence of poverty (i.e., wealth, or material well-being) or absence of hunger (i.e., satiety, or sufficient nourishment, or material well being). The analysis in the text remains equally applicable, whichever phrase or interpretation is used.

27. The widespread idea that all social matters can be socially, or even politically, more easily controlled than all physical or natural ones is false (unless eccentric definitions are used). Thus, language, a social phenomenon, is not easily controlled: no government has the power to make all Americans speak French, or even good English. Nor can political control make us all hate, or love, our government—a social phenomenon if there ever was one. But a government could have all American noses, or teeth, fixed, a "natural" or inborn physical matter. The contrary notion is derived from Karl Marx's distinction between "history" and "nature," a distinction from which Erich Fromm and other believers in "The

Sane Society" commended by "human nature" never recovered.

28. Here *liberté, egalité, fraternité* must share the blame. The first is up to the government; the second only in a narrow sense; the third not at all. The slogan makes *liberté*, which is government controlled, attractive by combining it with unrelated ideals which are not government controlled. They may be achieved independently. And they are often inconsistent with *liberté*.

29. An ideal, as distinguished from an actual, political system can by definition exclude anything one wishes to exclude. But since, unfortunately, actuality need not follow description and definition, it might be better to conform these to actuality. Confusion of an arbitrary blueprint, which simply excludes the problems for which it has no solution, with an actuality that cannot define problems away, must lead into disaster and has done so regularly. (See George Orwell, *Animal Farm* or *1984*.)

30. The classical Marxist reasoning is derived from what Isaiah Berlin (*op. cit.*) calls "positive freedom" (exalted particularly by some post-Kantian German philosophers): one is "free" if one does the "right" thing but not if one does not. "Freedom" becomes coercion to do the "right" thing. "Negative freedom," in contrast, leaves one able to do either thing, and coerced to do neither. (In a different usage "positive freedom" is identified, or confused, with ability. This usage has been discussed above on pp. 70–71.)

31. Pelagius, a contemporary of Saint Augustine, was a major heretic who denied hereditary sin or depravity, the fall from, and, therewith, the need for redemption through grace. Unlike Augustine, and like later Jesuits and finally the Protestants who had originally protested against them (only to become more Pelagian than the Jesuits ever were), Pelagius stressed the possibility of human progress and reason.

32. Even outside universities attempts to discourage illegitimate violence by raising the cost to perpetrators are few. Many well-meaning citizens concentrate on the rights of suspects and ignore the rights and needs of victims. It is odd but true that there are (quite legitimate) organizations to help released criminals, but none to help their victims.

haRpeR ⚜ toRchbooks

American Studies: General

HENRY ADAMS Degradation of the Democratic Dogma. ‡ Introduction by Charles Hirschfeld. TB/1450

LOUIS D. BRANDEIS: Other People's Money, and How the Bankers Use It. Ed. with Intro. by Richard M. Abrams TB/3081

HENRY STEELE COMMAGER, Ed.: The Struggle for Racial Equality TB/1300

CARL N. DEGLER: Out of Our Past: The Forces that Shaped Modern America CN/2

CARL N. DEGLER, Ed.: Pivotal Interpretations of American History
Vol. I TB/1240; Vol. II TB/1241

A. S. EISENSTADT, Ed.: The Craft of American History: Selected Essays
Vol. I TB/1255; Vol. II TB/1256

LAWRENCE H. FUCHS, Ed.: American Ethnic Politics TB/1368

MARCUS LEE HANSEN: The Atlantic Migration: 1607-1860. Edited by Arthur M. Schlesinger. Introduction by Oscar Handlin TB/1052

MARCUS LEE HANSEN: The Immigrant in American History. Edited with a Foreword by Arthur M. Schlesinger TB/1120

ROBERT L. HEILBRONER: The Limits of American Capitalism TB/1305

JOHN HIGHAM, Ed.: The Reconstruction of American History TB/1068

ROBERT H. JACKSON: The Supreme Court in the American System of Government TB/1106

JOHN F. KENNEDY: A Nation of Immigrants. Illus. Revised and Enlarged. Introduction by Robert F. Kennedy TB/1118

LEONARD W. LEVY, Ed.: American Constitutional Law: Historical Essays TB/1285

LEONARD W. LEVY, Ed.: Judicial Review and the Supreme Court TB/1296

LEONARD W. LEVY: The Law of the Commonwealth and Chief Justice Shaw: The Evolution of American Law, 1830-1860 TB/1309

GORDON K. LEWIS: Puerto Rico: Freedom and Power in the Caribbean. Abridged edition TB/1371

RICHARD B. MORRIS: Fair Trial: Fourteen Who Stood Accused, from Anne Hutchinson to Alger Hiss TB/1335

GUNNAR MYRDAL: An American Dilemma: The Negro Problem and Modern Democracy. Introduction by the Author.
Vol. I TB/1443; Vol. II TB/1444

GILBERT OSOFSKY, Ed.: The Burden of Race: A Documentary History of Negro-White Relations in America TB/1405

CONYERS READ, Ed.: The Constitution Reconsidered. Revised Edition. Preface by Richrd B. Morris TB/1384

ARNOLD ROSE: The Negro in America: The Condensed Version of Gunnar Myrdal's An American Dilemma. Second Edition TB/3048

JOHN E. SMITH: Themes in American Philosophy: Purpose, Experience and Community TB/1466

WILLIAM R. TAYLOR: Cavalier and Yankee: The Old South and American National Character TB/1474

American Studies: Colonial

BERNARD BAILYN: The New England Merchants in the Seventeenth Century TB/1149

ROBERT E. BROWN: Middle-Class Democracy and Revolution in Massachusetts, 1691-1780. New Introduction by Author TB/1413

JOSEPH CHARLES: The Origins of the American Party System TB/1049

HENRY STEELE COMMAGER & ELMO GIORDANETTI, Eds.: Was America a Mistake? An Eighteenth Century Controversy TB/1329

WESLEY FRANK CRAVEN: The Colonies in Transition: 1660-1712† TB/3084

CHARLES GIBSON: Spain in America † TB/3077

CHARLES GIBSON, Ed.: The Spanish Tradition in America + HR/1351

LAWRENCE HENRY GIPSON: The Coming of the Revolution: 1763-1775. † Illus. TB/3007

JACK P. GREENE, Ed.: Great Britain and the American Colonies: 1606-1763. + Introduction by the Author HR/1477

AUBREY C. LAND, Ed.: Bases of the Plantation Society + HR/1429

JOHN LANKFORD, Ed.: Captain John Smith's America: Selections from his Writings ‡ TB/3078

LEONARD W. LEVY: Freedom of Speech and Press in Early American History: Legacy of Suppression TB/1109

PERRY MILLER: Errand Into the Wilderness TB/1139

PERRY MILLER T. H. JOHNSON, Eds.: The Puritans: A Sourcebook of Their Writings
Vol. I TB/1093; Vol. II TB/1094

† The New American Nation Series, edited by Henry Steele Commager and Richard B. Morris.
‡ American Perspectives series, edited by Bernard Wishy and William E. Leuchtenburg.
a History of Europe series, edited by J. H. Plumb.
§ The Library of Religion and Culture, edited by Benjamin Nelson.
‖ Researches in the Social, Cultural, and Behavioral Sciences, edited by Benjamin Nelson.
Σ Harper Modern Science Series, edited by James A. Newman.
° Not for sale in Canada.
+ Documentary History of the United States series, edited by Richard B. Morris.
# Documentary History of Western Civilization series, edited by Eugene C. Black and Leonard W. Levy.
Λ The Economic History of the United States series, edited by Henry David et al.
¶ European Perspectives series, edited by Eugene C. Black.
** Contemporary Essays series, edited by Leonard W. Levy.
* The Stratum Series, edited by John Hale.

1

EDMUND S. MORGAN: The Puritan Family: *Religion and Domestic Relations in Seventeenth Century New England* TB/1227
RICHARD B. MORRIS: Government and Labor in Early America TB/1244
WALLACE NOTESTEIN: The English People on the Eve of Colonization: 1603-1630. † *Illus.* TB/3006
FRANCIS PARKMAN: The Seven Years War: *A Narrative Taken 'from* Montcalm and Wolfe, The Conspiracy of Pontiac, *and* A Half-Century of Conflict. *Edited by John H. McCallum* TB/3083
LOUIS B. WRIGHT: The Cultural Life of the American Colonies: 1607-1763. † *Illus.* TB/3005
YVES F. ZOLTVANY, Ed.: The French Tradition in America + HR/1425

American Studies: The Revolution to 1860

JOHN R. ALDEN: The American Revolution: 1775-1783. † *Illus.* TB/3011
MAX BELOFF, Ed.: The Debate on the American Revolution, 1761-1783: *A Sourcebook* TB/1225
RAY A. BILLINGTON: The Far Western Frontier: 1830-1860. † *Illus.* TB/3012
STUART BRUCHEY: The Roots of American Economic Growth, 1607-1861: *An Essay in Social Causation. New Introduction by the Author.* TB/1350
WHITNEY R. CROSS: The Burned-Over District: *The Social and Intellectual History of Enthusiastic Religion in Western New York, 1800-1850* TB/1242
NOBLE E. CUNNINGHAM, JR., Ed.: The Early Republic, 1789-1828 + HR/1394
GEORGE DANGERFIELD: The Awakening of American Nationalism, 1815-1828. † *Illus.* TB/3061
CLEMENT EATON: The Freedom-of-Thought Struggle in the Old South. *Revised and Enlarged. Illus.* TB/1150
CLEMENT EATON: The Growth of Southern Civilization, 1790-1860. † *Illus.* TB/3040
ROBERT H. FERRELL, Ed.: Foundations of American Diplomacy, 1775-1872 HR/1393
LOUIS FILLER: The Crusade against Slavery: 1830-1860. † *Illus.* TB/3029
DAVID H. FISCHER: The Revolution of American Conservatism: *The Federalist Party in the Era of Jeffersonian Democracy* TB/1449
WILLIAM W. FREEHLING, Ed.: The Nullification Era: *A Documentary Record* ‡ TB/3079
WILLIM W. FREEHLING: Prelude to Civil War: *The Nullification Controversy in South Carolina, 1816-1836* TB/1359
PAUL W. GATES: The Farmer's Age: *Agriculture, 1815-1860* △ TB/1398
FELIX GILBERT: The Beginnings of American Foreign Policy: *To the Farewell Address* TB/1200
ALEXANDER HAMILTON: The Reports of Alexander Hamilton. ‡ *Edited by Jacob E. Cooke* TB/3060
THOMAS JEFFERSON: Notes on the State of Virginia. ‡ *Edited by Thomas P. Abernethy* TB/3052
FORREST MCDONALD, Ed.: Confederation and Constitution, 1781-1789 + HR/1396
BERNARD MAYO: Myths and Men: *Patrick Henry, George Washington, Thomas Jefferson* TB/1108
JOHN C. MILLER: Alexander Hamilton and the Growth of the New Nation TB/3057
JOHN C. MILLER: The Federalist Era: 1789-1801. † *Illus.* TB/3027

RICHARD B. MORRIS, Ed.: Alexander Hamilton and the Founding of the Nation. *New Introduction by the Editor* TB/1448
RICHARD B. MORRIS: The American Revolution Reconsidered TB/1363
CURTIS P. NETTELS: The Emergence of a National Economy, 1775-1815 △ TB/1438
DOUGLASS C. NORTH & ROBERT PAUL THOMAS, Eds.: *The Growth of the American Economy to 1860* + TB/1352
R. B. NYE: The Cultural Life of the New Nation: 1776-1830. † *Illus.* TB/3026
GILBERT OSOFSKY, Ed.: Puttin' On Ole Massa: *The Slave Narratives of Henry Bibb, William Wells Brown, and Solomon Northup* ‡ TB/1432
JAMES PARTON: The Presidency of Andrew Jackson. *From Volume III of the* Life of Andrew Jackson. *Ed. with Intro. by Robert V. Remini* TB/3080
FRANCIS S. PHILBRICK: The Rise of the West, 1754-1830. † *Illus.* TB/3067
MARSHALL SMELSER: The Democratic Republic, 1801-1815 † TB/1406
TIMOTHY L. SMITH: Revivalism and Social Reform: *American Protestantism on the Eve of the Civil War* TB/1229
JACK M. SOSIN, Ed.: The Opening of the West + HR/1424
GEORGE ROGERS TAYLOR: The Transportation Revolution, 1815-1860 △ TB/1347
A. F. TYLER: Freedom's Ferment: *Phases of American Social History from the Revolution to the Outbreak of the Civil War. Illus.* TB/1074
GLYNDON G. VAN DEUSEN: The Jacksonian Era: 1828-1848. † *Illus.* TB/3028
LOUIS B. WRIGHT: Culture on the Moving Frontier TB/1053

American Studies: The Civil War to 1900

W. R. BROCK: An American Crisis: *Congress and Reconstruction, 1865-67* ° TB/1283
T. C. COCHRAN & WILLIAM MILLER: The Age of Enterprise: *A Social History of Industrial America* TB/1054
W. A. DUNNING: Reconstruction, Political and Economic: 1865-1877 TB/1073
HAROLD U. FAULKNER: Politics, Reform and Expansion: 1890-1900. † *Illus.* TB/3020
GEORGE M. FREDRICKSON: The Inner Civil War: *Northern Intellectuals and the Crisis of the Union* TB/1358
JOHN A. GARRATY: The New Commonwealth, 1877-1890 † TB/1410
JOHN A. GARRATY, Ed.: The Transformation of American Society, 1870-1890 + HR/1395
HELEN HUNT JACKSON: A Century of Dishonor: *The Early Crusade for Indian Reform.* † *Edited by Andrew F. Rolle* TB/3063
ALBERT D. KIRWAN: Revolt of the Rednecks: *Mississippi Politics, 1876-1925* TB/1199
ARTHUR MANN: Yankee Reforms in the Urban Age: *Social Reform in Boston, 1800-1900* TB/1247
ARNOLD M. PAUL: Conservative Crisis and the Rule of Law: *Attitudes of Bar and Bench, 1887-1895. New Introduction by Author* TB/1415
JAMES S. PIKE: The Prostrate State: *South Carolina under Negro Government.* ‡ *Intro. by Robert F. Durden* TB/3085
WHITELAW REID: After the War: *A Tour of the Southern States, 1865-1866.* ‡ *Edited by C. Vann Woodward* TB/3066
FRED A. SHANNON: The Farmer's Last Frontier: *Agriculture, 1860-1897* TB/1348

W. ARTHUR LEWIS: Economic Survey, 1919-1939
TB/1446
W. ARTHUR LEWIS: The Principles of Economic
Planning. *New Introduction by the Author°*
TB/1436
ROBERT GREEN MC CLOSKEY: American Conserva-
tism in the Age of Enterprise   TB/1137
PAUL MANTOUX: The Industrial Revolution in
the Eighteenth Century: *An Outline of the
Beginnings of the Modern Factory System in
England°*   TB/1079
WILLIAM MILLER, Ed.: Men in Business: *Essays
on the Historical Role of the Entrepreneur*
TB/1081
GUNNAR MYRDAL: An International Economy.
New Introduction by the Author   TB/1445
RICHARD S. WECKSTEIN, Ed.: Expansion of World
Trade and the Growth of National Econ-
omies **   TB/1373

Historiography and History of Ideas

HERSCHEL BAKER: The Image of Man: *A Study
of the Idea of Human Dignity in Classical
Antiquity, the Middle Ages, and the Renais-
sance*   TB/1047
J. BRONOWSKI & BRUCE MAZLISH: The Western
Intellectual Tradition: *From Leonardo to
Hegel*   TB/3001
EDMUND BURKE: On Revolution. Ed. by Robert
A. Smith   TB/1401
WILHELM DILTHEY: Pattern and Meaning in His-
tory: *Thoughts on History and Society.°*
Edited with an Intro. by H. P. Rickman
TB/1075
ALEXANDER GRAY: The Socialist Tradition: *Moses
to Lenin °*   TB/1375
J. H. HEXTER: More's Utopia: *The Biography of
an Idea. Epilogue by the Author*   TB/1195
H. STUART HUGHES: History as Art and as
Science: *Twin Vistas on the Past*   TB/1207
ARTHUR O. LOVEJOY: The Great Chain of Being:
A Study of the History of an Idea TB/1009
JOSE ORTEGA Y GASSET: The Modern Theme.
Introduction by Jose Ferrater Mora TB/1038
RICHARD H. POPKIN: The History of Scepticism
from Erasmus to Descartes. *Revised Edition*
TB/1391
G. J. RENIER: History: *Its Purpose and Method*
TB/1209
MASSIMO SALVADORI, Ed.: Modern Socialism #
HR/1374
BRUNO SNELL: The Discovery of the Mind: *The
Greek Origins of European Thought* TB/1018
W. WARREN WAGER, ed.: European Intellectual
History Since Darwin and Marx   TB/1297
W. H. WALSH: Philosophy of History: In Intro-
duction   TB/1020

History: General

HANS KOHN: The Age of Nationalism: *The
First Era of Global History*   TB/1380
BERNARD LEWIS: The Arabs in History TB/1029
BERNARD LEWIS: The Middle East and the
West °   TB/1274

History: Ancient

A. ANDREWS: The Greek Tyrants   TB/1103
ERNST LUDWIG EHRLICH: A Concise History of
Israel: *From the Earliest Times to the De-
struction of the Temple in A.D. 70°* TB/128

THEODOR H. GASTER: Thespis: *Ritual Myth and
Drama in the Ancient Near East*   TB/1281
MICHAEL GRANT: Ancient History °   TB/1190
A. H. M. JONES, Ed.: A History of Rome
through the Fifgth Century # *Vol. I: The
Republic*   HR/1364
Vol. II The Empire: HR/1460
SAMUEL NOAH KRAMER: Sumerian Mythology
TB/1055
NAPHTALI LEWIS & MEYER REINHOLD, Eds.:
Roman Civilization *Vol. I: The Republic*
TB/1231
Vol. II: The Empire   TB/1232

History: Medieval

MARSHALL W. BALDWIN, Ed.: Christianity
Through the 13th Century #   HR/1468
MARC BLOCH: Land and Work in Medieval
Europe. *Translated by J. E. Anderson*
TB/1452
HELEN CAM: England Before Elizabeth TB/1026
NORMAN COHN: The Pursuit of the Millennium:
*Revolutionary Messianism in Medieval and
Reformation Europe*   TB/1037
G. G. COULTON: Medieval Village, Manor, and
Monastery   HR/1022
HEINRICH FICHTENAU: The Carolingian Empire:
*The Age of Charlemagne. Translated with an
Introduction by Peter Munz*   TB/1142
GALBERT OF BRUGES: The Murder of Charles the
Good: *A Contemporary Record of Revolu-
tionary Change in 12th Century Flanders.
Translated with an Introduction by James
Bruce Ross*   TB/1311
F. L. GANSHOF: Feudalism   TB/1058
F. L. GANSHOF: The Middle Ages: *A History of
International Relations. Translated by Rémy
Hall*   TB/1411
DENYS HAY: The Medieval Centuries ° TB/1192
DAVID HERLIHY, Ed.: Medieval Culture and So-
ciety #   HR/1340
J. M. HUSSEY: The Byzantine World   TB/1057
ROBERT LATOUCHE: The Birth of Western Econ-
omy: *Economic Aspects of the Dark Ages °*
TB/1290
HENRY CHARLES LEA: The Inquisition of the
Middle Ages. || *Introduction by Walter
Ullmann*   TB/1456
FERDINARD LOT: The End of the Ancient World
and the Beginnings of the Middle Ages. *In-
troduction by Glanville Downey*   TB/1044
H. R. LOYN: The Norman Conquest   TB/1457
GUIBERT DE NOGENT: Self and Society in
Medieval France: *The Memoirs of Guilbert de
Nogent.* || Edited by John F. Benton TB/1471
MARSILIUS OF PADUA: The Defender of Peace.
*The Defensor Pacis. Translated with an In-
troduction by Alan Gewirth*   TB/1310
CHARLES PETET-DUTAILLIS: The Feudal Monarchy
in France and England: *From the Tenth to
the Thirteenth Century °*   TB/1165
STEVEN RUNCIMAN: A History of the Crusades
*Vol. I: The First Crusade and the Founda-
tion of the Kingdom of Jerusalem. Illus.*
TB/1143
*Vol. II: The Kingdom of Jerusalem and the
Frankish East 1100-1187. Illus.*   TB/1243
*Vol. III: The Kingdom of Acre and the
Later Crusades. Illus.*   TB/1298
J. M. WALLACE-HADRILL: The Barbarian West:
The Early Middle Ages, A.D. 400-1000
TB/1061

JACOB BURCKHARDT: The Civilization of the Renaissance in Italy. *Introduction by Benjamin Nelson and Charles Trinkaus. Illus.* Vol. I TB/40; Vol. II TB/41

JOHN CALVIN & JACOPO SADOLETO: A Reformation Debate. *Edited by John C. Olin* TB/1239

FEDERICO CHABOD: Machiavelli and the Renaissance TB/1193

THOMAS CROMWELL: Thomas Cromwell. *Selected Letters on Church and Commonwealth, 1523-1540.* ¶ *Ed. with an Intro. by Arthur J. Slavin* TB/1462

R. TREVOR DAVIES: The Golden Century of Spain, 1501-1621 ° TB/1194

J. H. ELLIOTT: Europe Divided, 1559-1598 *a* ° TB/1414

G. R. ELTON: Reformation Europe, 1517-1559 ° *a* TB/1270

DESIDERIUS ERASMUS: Christian Humanism and the Reformation: *Selected Writings. Edited and Translated by John C. Olin* TB/1166

DESIDERIUS ERASMUS: Erasmus and His Age: *Selected Letters. Edited with an Introduction by Hans J. Hillerbrand. Translated by Marcus A. Haworth* TB/1461

WALLACE K. FERGUSON et al.: Facets of the Renaissance TB/1098

WALLACE K. FERGUSON et al.: The Renaissance: *Six Essays. Illus.* TB/1084

FRANCESCO GUICCIARDINI: History of Florence. *Translated with an Introduction and Notes by Mario Domandi* TB/1470

WERNER L. GUNDERSHEIMER, Ed.: French Humanism, 1470-1600. * *Illus.* TB/1473

MARIE BOAS HALL, Ed.: Nature and Nature's Laws: *Documents of the Scientific Revolution* # HR/1420

HANS J. HILLERBRAND, Ed., The Protestant Reformation HR/1342

JOHAN HUIZINGA: Erasmus and the Age of Reformation. *Illus.* TB/19

JOEL HURSTFIELD: The Elizabethan Nation TB/1312

JOEL HURSTFIELD, Ed.: The Reformation Crisis TB/1267

PAUL OSKAR KRISTELLER: Renaissance Thought: *The Classic, Scholastic, and Humanist Strains* TB/1048

PAUL OSKAR KRISTELLER: Renaissance Thought II: *Papers on Humanism and the Arts* TB/1163

PAUL O. KRISTELLER & PHILIP P. WIENER, Eds.: Renaissance Essays TB/1392

DAVID LITTLE: Religion, Order and Law: *A Study in Pre-Revolutionary England.* § *Preface by R. Bellah* TB/1418

NICCOLO MACHIAVELLI: History of Florence and of the Affairs of Italy: *From the Earliest Times to the Death of Lorenzo the Magnificent. Introduction by Felix Gilbert* TB/1027

ALFRED VON MARTIN: Sociology of the Renaissance. ° *Introduction by W. K. Ferguson* TB/1099

GARRETT MATTINGLY et al.: Renaissance Profiles. *Edited by J. H. Plumb* TB/1162

J. E. NEALE: The Age of Catherine de Medici ° TB/1085

J. H. PARRY: The Establishment of the European Hegemony: 1415-1715: *Trade and Exploration in the Age of the Renaissance* TB/1045

J. H. PARRY, Ed.: The European Reconnaissance: *Selected Documents* # HR/1345

BUONACCORSO PITTI & GREGORIO DATI: Two Memoirs of Renaissance Florence: *The Diaries of Buonaccorso Pitti and Gregorio Dati. Edited with Intro. by Gene Brucker. Trans. by Julia Martines* TB/1333

J. H. PLUMB: The Italian Renaissance: *A Concise Survey of Its History and Culture* TB/1161

A. F. POLLARD: Henry VIII. *Introduction by A. G. Dickens.* ° TB/1249

RICHARD H. POPKIN: The History of Scepticism from Erasmus to Descartes TB/1391

PAOLO ROSSI: Philosophy, Technology, and the Arts, in the Early Modern Era 1400-1700. || *Edited by Benjamin Nelson. Translated by Salvator Attanasio* TB/1458

FERDINAND SCHEVILL: The Medici. *Illus.* TB/1010

FERDINAND SCHEVILL: Medieval and Renaissance Florence. *Illus.* Vol. I: *Medieval Florence* TB/1090

Vol. II: The Coming of Humanism and the Age of the Medici TB/1091

R. H. TAWNEY: The Agrarian Problem in the Sixteenth Century. *Intro. by Lawrence Stone* TB/1315

H. R. TREVOR-ROPER: The European Witch-craze of the Sixteenth and Seventeenth Centuries and Other Essays ° TB/1416

VESPASIANO: Rennaissance Princes, Popes, and XVth Century: *The Vespasiano Memoirs. Introduction by Myron P. Gilmore. Illus.* TB/1111

RENE ALBRECHT-CARRIE, Ed.: The Concert of Europe # HR/1341

MAX BELOFF: The Age of Absolutism, 1660-1815 TB/1062

OTTO VON BISMARCK: Reflections and Reminiscences. *Ed. with Intro. by Theodore S. Hamerow* ¶ TB/1357

EUGENE C. BLACK, Ed.: British Politics in the Nineteenth Century # HR/1427

EUGENE C. BLACK, Ed.: European Political History, 1815-1870: *Aspects of Liberalism* ¶ TB/1331

ASA BRIGGS: The Making of Modern England, 1783-1867: *The Age of Improvement* ° TB/1203

ALAN BULLOCK: Hitler, A Study in Tyranny. ° *Revised Edition. Illus.* TB/1123

EDMUND BURKE: On Revolution. *Ed. by Robert A. Smith* TB/1401

E. R. CARR: International Relations Between the Two World Wars. 1919-1939 ° TB/1279

E. H. CARR: The Twenty Years' Crisis, 1919-1939: *An Introduction to the Study of International Relations* ° TB/1122

GORDON A. CRAIG: From Bismarck to Adenauer: *Aspects of German Statecraft. Revised Edition* TB/1171

LESTER G. CROCKER, Ed.: The Age of Enlightenment # HR/1423

DENIS DIDEROT: The Encyclopedia: *Selections. Edited and Translated with Introduction by Stephen Gendzier* TB/1299

JACQUES DROZ: Europe between Revolutions, 1815-1848. ° *a Trans. by Robert Baldick* TB/1346

JOHANN GOTTLIEB FICHTE: Addresses to the German Nation. *Ed. with Intro. by George A. Kelly* ¶ TB/1366

ROBERT & ELBORG FORSTER, Eds.: European Society in the Eighteenth Century # HR/1404

C. C. GILLISPIE: Genesis and Geology: *The Decades before Darwin* § TB/51

Literature & Literary Criticism

Philosophy

ERNST CASSIRER: Rousseau, Kant and Goethe. *Intro. by Peter Gay* TB/1092
FREDERICK COPLESTON, S. J.: Medieval Philosophy TB/376
F. M. CORNFORD: From Religion to Philosophy: *A Study in the Origins of Western Speculation* § TB/20
WILFRID DESAN: The Tragic Finale: *An Essay on the Philosophy of Jean-Paul Sartre* TB/1030
MARVIN FARBER: The Aims of Phenomenology: *The Motives, Methods, and Impact of Husserl's Thought* TB/1291
MARVIN FARBER: Basic Issues of Philosophy: *Experience, Reality, and Human Values* TB/1344
MARVIN FARBERS: Phenomenology and Existence: *Towards a Philosophy within Nature* TB/1295
PAUL FRIEDLANDER: `Plato: *An Introduction* TB/2017
MICHAEL GELVEN: A Commentary on Heidegger's "Being and Time" TB/1464
J. GLENN GRAY: Hegel and Greek Thought TB/1409
W. K. C. GUTHRIE: The Greek Philosophers: *From Thales to Aristotle* ° TB/1008
G. W. F. HEGEL: On Art, Religion Philosophy: *Introductory Lectures to the Realm of Absolute Spirit.* || *Edited with an Introduction by J. Glenn Gray* TB/1463
G. W. F. HEGEL: Phenomenology of Mind. ° || *Introduction by George Lichtheim* TB/1303
MARTIN HEIDEGGER: Discourse on Thinking. *Translated with a Preface by John M. Anderson and E. Hans Freund. Introduction by John M. Anderson* TB/1459
F. H. HEINEMANN: Existentialism and the Modern Predicament TB/28
WERER HEISENBERG: Physics and Philosophy: *The Revolution in Modern Science. Intro. by F. S. C. Northrop* TB/549
EDMUND HUSSERL: Phenomenology and the Crisis of Philosophy. § *Translated with an Introduction by Quentin Lauer* TB/1170
IMMANUEL KANT: Groundwork of the Metaphysic of Morals. *Translated and Analyzed by H. J. Paton* TB/1159
IMMANUEL KANT: Lectures on Ethics. § *Introduction by Lewis White Beck* TB/105
WALTER KAUFMANN, Ed.: Religion From Tolstoy to Camus: *Basic Writings on Religious Truth and Morals* TB/123
QUENTIN LAUER: Phenomenology: *Its Genesis and Prospect. Preface by Aron Gurwitsch* TB/1169
MAURICE MANDELBAUM: The Problem of Historical Knowledge: *An Answer to Relativism* TB/1198
H. J. PATON: The Categorical Imperative: *A Study in Kant's Moral Philosophy* TB/1325
MICHAEL POLANYI: Personal Knowledge: *Towards a Post-Critical Philosophy* TB/1158
KARL R. POPPER: Conjectures and Refutations: *The Growth of Scientific Knowledge* TB/1376
WILLARD VAN ORMAN QUINE: Elementary Logic *Revised Edition* TB/577
WILLARD VAN ORMAN QUINE: From a Logical Point of View: *Logico-Philosophical Essays* TB/566
JOHN E. SMITH: Themes in American Philosophy: *Purpose, Experience and Community* TB/1466
MORTON WHITE: Foundations of Historical Knowledge TB/1440
WILHELM WINDELBAND: A History of Philosophy *Vol. I: Greek, Roman, Medieval* TB/38 *Vol. II: Renaissance, Enlightenment, Modern* TB/39

LUDWIG WITTGENSTEIN: The Blue and Brown Books ° TB/1211
LUDWIG WITTGENSTEIN: Notebooks, 1914-1916 TB/1441

Political Science & Government

C. E. BLACK: The Dynamics of Modernization: *A Study in Comparative History* TB/1321
DENIS W. BROGAN: Politics in America. *New Introduction by the Author* TB/1469
CRANE BRINTON: English Political Thought in the Nineteenth Century TB/1071
ROBERT CONQUEST: Power and Policy in the USSR: *The Study of Soviet Dynastics* ° TB/1307
ROBERT A. DAHL & CHARLES E. LINDBLOM: Politics, Economics, and Welfare: *Planning and Politico-Economic Systems Resolved into Basic Social Processes* TB/1277
HANS KOHN: Political Ideologies of the 20th Century TB/1277
ROY C. MACRIDIS, Ed.: Political Parties: *Contemporary Trends and Ideas* ** TB/1322
ROBERT GREEN MC CLOSKEY: American Conservatism in the Age of Enterprise, 1865-1910 TB/1137
MARSILIUS OF PADUA: The Defender of Peace. *The Defensor Pacis. Translated with an Introduction by Alan Gewirth* TB/1310
KINGSLEY MARTIN: French Liberal Thought in the Eighteenth Century: *A Study of Political Ideas from Bayle to Condorcet* TB/1114
BARRINGTON MOORE, JR.:Political Power and Social Theory: *Seven Studies* || TB/1221
BARRINGTON MOORE, JR.: Soviet Politics—The Dilemma of Power: *The Role of Ideas in Social Change* || TB/1222
BARRINGTON MOORE, JR.: Terror and Progress—USSR: *Some Sources of Change and Stability* TB/1266
JOHN B. MORRALL: Political Thought in Medieval Times TB/1076
KARL R. POPPER: The Open Society and Its Enemies *Vol. I: The Spell of Plato* TB/1101 *Vol. II: The High Tide of Prophecy: Hegel, Marx, and the Aftermath* TB/1102
CONYERS READ, Ed.: The Constitution Reconsidered. *Revised Edition, Preface by Richard B. Morris* TB/1384
JOHN P. ROCHE, Ed.: Origins of American Political Thought: *Selected Readings* TB/1301
JOHN P. ROCHE, Ed.: American Political Thought: *From Jefferson to Progressivism* TB/1332
HENRI DE SAINT-SIMON: Social Organization, The Science of Man, and Other Writings. || *Edited and Translated with an Introduction by Felix Markham* TB/1152
CHARLES SCHOTTLAND, Ed.: The Welfare State ** TB/1323
JOSEPH A. SCHUMPETER: Capitalism, Socialism and Democracy TB/3008

Psychology

ALFRED ADLER: The Individual Psychology of Alfred Adler: *A Systematic Presentation in Selections from His Writings. Edited by Heinz L. & Rowena R. Ansbacher* TB/1154
LUDWIG BINSWANGER: Being-in-the-World: *Selected Papers.* || *Trans. with Intro. by Jacob Needleman* TB/1365
HADLEY CANTRIL: The Invasion from Mars: *A Study in the Psychology of Panic* || TB/1282
MIRCEA ELIADE: Cosmos and History: *The Myth of the Eternal Return* § TB/2050
MIRCEA ELIADE: Myth and Reality TB/1369

MIRCEA ELIADE: Myths, Dreams and Mysteries: *The Encounter Between Contemporary Faiths and Archaic Realities* § TB/1320
MIRCEA ELIADE: Rites and Symbols of Initiation: *The Mysteries of Birth and Rebirth* § TB/1236
HERBERT FINGARETTE: The Self in Transformation: *Psychoanalysis, Philosophy and the Life of the Spirit* || 1B/1177
SIGMUND FREUD: On Creativity and the Unconscious: *Papers on the Psychology of Art, Literature, Love, Religion.* § *Intro. by Benjamin Nelson* TB/45
J. GLENN GRAY: The Warriors: *Reflections on Men in Battle. Introduction by Hannah Arendt* TB/1294
WILLIAM JAMES: Psychology: *The Briefer Course. Edited with an Intro. by Gordon Allport* TB/1034
C. G. JUNG: Psychological Reflections. *Ed. by J. Jacobi* TB/2001
KARL MENNINGER, M.D.: Theory of Psychoanalytic Technique TB/1144
JOHN H. SCHAAR: Escape from Authority: *The Perspectives of Erich Fromm* TB/1155
MUZAFER SHERIF: The Psychology of Social Norms. *Introduction by Gardner Murphy* TB/3072
HELLMUT WILHELM: Change: *Eight Lectures on the* I *Ching* TB/2019

Religion: Ancient and Classical, Biblical and Judaic Traditions

W. F. ALBRIGHT: The Biblical Period from Abraham to Ezra TB/102
SALO W. BARON: Modern Nationalism and Religion TB/818
C. K. BARRETT, Ed.: The New Testament Background: *Selected Documents* TB/86
MARTIN BUBER: Eclipse of God: *Studies in the Relation Between Religion and Philosophy* TB/12
MARTIN BUBER: Hasidism and Modern Man. *Edited and Translated by Maurice Friedman* TB/839
MARTIN BUBER: The Knowledge of Man. *Edited with an Introduction by Maurice Friedman. Translated by Maurice Friedman and Ronald Gregor Smith* TB/135
MARTIN BUBER: Moses. *The Revelation and the Covenant* TB/837
MARTIN BUBER: The Origin and Meaning of Hasidism. *Edited and Translated by Maurice Friedman* TB/835
MARTIN BUBER: The Prophetic Faith TB/73
MARTIN BUBER: Two Types of Faith: *Interpenetration of Judaism and Christianity* ° TB/75
MALCOLM L. DIAMOND: Martin Buber: *Jewish Existentialist* TB/840
M. S. ENSLIN: Christian Beginnings TB/5
M. S. ENSLIN: The Literature of the Christian Movement TB/6
ERNST LUDWIG EHRLICH: A Concise History of Israel: *From the Earliest Times to the Destruction of the Temple in A.D. 70* ° TB/128
HENRI FRANKFORT: Ancient Egyptian Religion: *An Interpretation* TB/77
ABRAHAM HESCHEL: The Earth Is the Lord's & The Sabbath. *Two Essays* TB/828
ABRAHAM HESCHEL: God in Search of Man: *A Philosophy of Judaism* TB/807
ABRAHAM HESCHEL: Man Is not Alone: *A Philosophy of Religion* TB/838
ABRAHAM HESCHEL: The Prophets: *An Introduction* TB/1421

T. J. MEEK: Hebrew Origins TB/69
JAMES MUILENBURG: The Way of Israel: *Biblical Faith and Ethics* TB/133
H. J. ROSE: Religion in Greece and Rome TB/55
H. H. ROWLEY: The Growth of the Old Testament TB/107
D. WINTON THOMAS, Ed.: Documents from Old Testament Times TB/85

Religion: General Christianity

ROLAND H. BAINTON: Christendom: *A Short History of Christianity and Its Impact on Western Civilization. Illus.* Vol. I TB/131; Vol. II TB/132
JOHN T. MCNEILL: Modern Christian Movements. *Revised Edition* TB/1402
ERNST TROELTSCH: The Social Teaching of the Christian Churches. *Intro. by H. Richard Niebuhr* Vol. TB/71; Vol. II TB/72

Religion: Early Christianity Through
Reformation

ANSELM OF CANTERBURY: Truth, Freedom, and Evil: *Three Philosophical Dialogues. Edited and Translated by Jasper Hopkins and Herbert Richardson* TB/317
MARSHALL W. BALDWIN, Ed.: Christianity through the 13th Century # HR/1468
W. D. DAVIES: Paul and Rabbinic Judaism: *Some Rabbinic Elements in Pauline Theology. Revised Edition* ° TB/146
ADOLF DEISSMANN: Paul: *A Study in Social and Religious History* TB/15
JOHANNES ECKHART: Meister Eckhart: *A Modern Translation by R. Blakney* TB/8
EDGAR J. GOODSPEED: A Life of Jesus TB/1
ROBERT M. GRANT: Gnosticism and Early Christianity TB/136
WILLIAM HALLER: The Rise of Puritanism TB/22
GERHART B. LADNER: The Idea of Reform: *Its Impact on the Christian Thought and Action in the Age of the Fathers* TB/149
ARTHUR DARBY NOCK: Early Gentile Christianity and Its Hellenistic Background TB/111
ARTHUR DARBY NOCK: St. Paul ° TR/104
GORDON RUPP: Luther's Progress to the Diet of Worms ° TB/120

Religion: The Protestant Tradition

KARL BARTH: Church Dogmatics: *A Selection. Intro. by H. Gollwitzer. Ed. by G. W. Bromiley* TB/95
KARL BARTH: Dogmatics in Outline TB/56
KARL BARTH: The Word of God and the Word of Man TB/13
HERBERT BRAUN, et al.: God and Christ: *Existence and Province. Volume 5 of* Journal for Theology and the Church, *edited by Robert W. Funk and Gerhard Ebeling* TB/255
WHITNEY R. CROSS: The Burned-Over District: *The Social and Intellectual History of Enthusiastic Religion in Western New York, 1800-1850* TB/1242
NELS F. S. FERRE: Swedish Contributions to Modern Theology. *New Chapter by William A. Johnson* TB/147
WILLIAM R. HUTCHISON, Ed.: American Protestant Thought: *The Liberal Era* ‡ TB/1385
ERNST KASEMANN, et al.: Distinctive Protestant and Catholic Themes Reconsidered. *Volume 3 of Journal for Theology and the Church,*

edited by Robert W. Funk and Gerhard Ebeling TB/253

SOREN KIERKEGAARD: On Authority and Revelation: *The Book on Adler, or a Cycle of Ethico-Religious Essays. Introduction by F. Sontag* TB/139

SOREN KIERKEGAARD: Crisis in the Life of an Actress, *and Other Essays on Drama. Translated with an Introduction by Stephen Crites* TB/145

SOREN KIERKEGAARD: Edifying Discourses. *Edited with an Intro. by Paul Holmer* TB/32

SOREN KIERKEGAARD: The Journals of Kierkegaard. ° *Edited with an Intro. by Alexander Dru* TB/52

SOREN KIERKEGAARD: The Point of View for My Work as an Author: *A Report to History.* § *Preface by Benjamin Nelson* TB/88

SOREN KIERKEGAARD: The Present Age. § *Translated and edited by Alexander Dru. Introduction by Walter Kaufmann* TB/94

SOREN KIERKEGAARD: Purity of Heart. *Trans. by Douglas Steere* TB/4

SOREN KIERKEGAARD: Repetition: *An Essay in Experimental Psychology* § TB/117

SOREN KIERKEGAARD: Works of Love: *Some Christian Reflections in the Form of Discourses* TB/122

WILLIAM G. MCLOUGHLIN, Ed.: The American Evangelicals: 1800-1900: *An Anthology* TB/1382

WOLFHART PANNENBERG, et al.: History and Hermeneutic. *Volume 4 of* Journal for Theology and the Church, *edited by Robert W. Funk and Gerhard Ebeling* TB/254

JAMES M. ROBINSON, et al.: The Bultmann School of Biblical Interpretation: New Directions? *Volume 1 of* Journal for Theology and the Church, *edited by Robert W. Funk and Gerhard Ebeling* TB/251

F. SCHLEIERMACHER: The Christian Faith. *Introduction by Richard R. Niebuhr.*
Vol. I TB/108; Vol. II TB/109

F. SCHLEIERMACHER: On Religion: *Speeches to Its Cultured Despisers. Intro. by Rudolf Otto* TB/36

TIMOTHY L. SMITH: Revivalism and Social Reform: *American Protestantism on the Eve of the Civil War* TB/1229

PAUL TILLICH: Dynamics of Faith TB/42

PAUL TILLICH: Morality and Beyond TB/142

EVELYN UNDERHILL: Worship TB/10

Religion: The Roman & Eastern Christian Traditions

A. ROBERT CAPONIGRI, Ed.: Modern Catholic Thinkers II: *The Church and the Political Order* TB/307

G. P. FEDOTOV: The Russian Religious Mind: *Kievan Christianity, the tenth to the thirteenth Centuries* TB/370

GABRIEL MARCEL: Being and Having: *An Existential Diary. Introduction by James Collins* TB/310

GABRIEL MARCEL: Homo Viator: *Introduction to a Metaphysic of Hope* TB/397

Religion: Oriental Religions

TOR ANDRAE: Mohammed: *The Man and His Faith* § TB/62

EDWARD CONZE: Buddhism: *Its Essence and Development.* ° *Foreword by Arthur Waley* TB/58

EDWARD CONZE: Buddhist Meditation TB/1442

EDWARD CONZE et al, Editors: Buddhist Texts through the Ages TB/113

ANANDA COOMARASWAMY: Buddha and the Gospel of Buddhism TB/119

H. G. CREEL: Confucius and the Chinese Way TB/63

FRANKLIN EDGERTON, Trans. & Ed.: The Bhagavad Gita TB/115

SWAMI NIKHILANANDA, Trans. & Ed.: The Upanishads TB/114

D. T. SUZUKI: On Indian Mahayana Buddhism. ° *Ed. with Intro. by Edward Conze.* TB/1403

Religion: Philosophy, Culture, and Society

NICOLAS BERDYAEV: The Destiny of Man TB/61

RUDOLF BULTMANN: History and Eschatology: *The Presence of Eternity* ° TB/91

RUDOLF BULTMANN AND FIVE CRITICS: Kerygma and Myth: *A Theological Debate* TB/80

RUDOLF BULTMANN and KARL KUNDSIN: Form Criticism: *Two Essays on New Testament Research. Trans. by F. C. Grant* TB/96

WILLIAM A. CLEBSCH & CHARLES R. JAEKLE: Pastoral Care in Historical Perspective: *An Essay with Exhibits* TB/148

FREDERICK FERRÉ: Language, Logic and God. *New Preface by the Author* TB/1407

LUDWIG FEUERBACH: The Essence of Christianity. § *Introduction by Karl Barth. Foreword by H. Richard Niebuhr* TB/11

ADOLF HARNACK: What Is Christianity? § *Introduction by Rudolf Bultmann* TB/17

KYLE HASELDEN: The Racial Problem in Christian Perspective TB/116

MARTIN HEIDEGGER: Discourse on Thinking. *Translated with a Preface by John M. Anderson and E. Hans Freund. Introduction by John M. Anderson* TB/1459

IMMANUEL KANT: Religion Within the Limits of Reason Alone. § *Introduction by Theodore M. Greene and John Silber* TB/FG

WALTER KAUFMANN, Ed.: Religion from Tolstoy to Camus: *Basic Writings on Religious Truth and Morals. Enlarged Edition* TB/123

H. RICHARD NIEBUHR: Christ and Culture TB/3

H. RICHARD NIEBUHR: The Kingdom of God in America TB/49

ANDERS NYGREN: Agape and Eros. *Translated by Philip S. Watson* ° TB/1430

JOHN H. RANDALL, JR.: The Meaning of Religion for Man. *Revised with New Intro. by the Author* TB/1379

WALTER RAUSCHENBUSCHS Christianity and the Social Crisis. ‡ *Edited by Robert D. Cross* TB/3059

Science and Mathematics

JOHN TYLER BONNER: The Ideas of Biology. Σ *Illus.* TB/570

W. E. LE GROS CLARK: The Antecedents of Man: *An Introduction to the Evolution of the Primates.* ° *Illus.* TB/559

ROBERT E. COKER: Streams, Lakes, Ponds. *Illus.* TB/586

ROBERT E. COKER: This Great and Wide Sea: *An Introduction to Oceanography and Marine Biology. Illus.* TB/551

W. H. DOWDESWELL: Animal Ecology. *61 illus.* TB/543

C. V. DURELL: Readable Relativity. *Foreword by Freeman J. Dyson* TB/530

GEORGE GAMOW: Biography of Physics. Σ *Illus.* TB/567

F. K. HARE: The Restless Atmosphere TB/560

J. R. PIERCE: Symbols, Signals and Noise: *The Nature and Process of Communication* Σ TB/574

WILLARD VAN ORMAN QUINE: Mathematical Logic TB/558

Science: History

MARIE BOAS: The Scientific Renaissance, 1450-1630 ° TB/583

STEPHEN TOULMIN & JUNE GOODFIELD: The Architecture of Matter: *The Physics, Chemistry and Physiology of Matter, Both Animate and Inanimate, as it has Evolved since the Beginnings of Science* TB/584

STEPHEN TOULMIN & JUNE GOODFIELD: The Discovery TB/576

STEPHEN TOULMIN & JUNE GOODFIELD: The Fabric of the Heavens: *The Development of Astronomy and Dynamics* TB/579

Science: Philosophy

J. M. BOCHENSKI: The Methods of Contemporary Thought. *Tr. by Peter Caws* TB/1377

J. BRONOWSKI: Science and Human Values. *Revised and Enlarged. Illus.* TB/505

WERNER HEISENBERG: Physics and Philosophy: *The Revolution in Modern Science. Introduction by F. S. C. Northrop* TB/549

KARL R. POPPER: Conjectures and Refutations: *The Growth of Scientific Knowledge* TB/1376

KARL R. POPPER: The Logic of Scientific Discovery TB/1376

STEPHEN TOULMIN: Foresight and Understanding: *An Enquiry into the Aims of Science. Foreword by Jacques Barzun* TB/564

STEPHEN TOULMIN: The Philosophy of Science: *An Introduction* TB/513

Sociology and Anthropology

REINHARD BENDIX: Work and Authority in Industry: *Ideologies of Management in the Course of Industrialization* TB/3035

BERNARD BERELSON, Ed.: The Behavioral Sciences Today TB/1127

JOSEPH B. CASAGRANDE, Ed.: In the Company of Man: *Twenty Portraits of Anthropological Informants. Illus.* TB/3047

KENNETH B. CLARK: Dark Ghetto: *Dilemmas of Social Power. Foreword by Gunnar Myrdal* TB/1317

KENNETH CLARK & JEANNETTE HOPKINS: A Relevant War Against Poverty: *A Study of Community Action Programs and Observable Social Change* TB/1480

LEWIS COSER, Ed.: Political Sociology TB/1293

ROSE L. COSER, Ed.: Life Cycle and Achievement in America ** TB/1434

ALLISON DAVIS & JOHN DOLLARD: Children of Bondage: *The Personality Development of Negro Youth in the Urban South* || TB/3049

PETER F. DRUCKER: The New Society: *The Anatomy of Industrial Order* TB/1082

CORA DU BOIS: The People of Alor. *With a Preface by the Author*
Vol. I *Illus.* TB/1042; Vol. II TB/1043

EMILE DURKHEIM et al.: Essays on Sociology and Philosophy: *with Appraisals of Durkheim's Life and Thought.* || *Edited by Kurt H. Wolff* TB/1151

LEON FESTINGER, HENRY W. RIECKEN, STANLEY SCHACHTER: When Prophecy Fails: *A Social and Psychological Study of a Modern Group that Predicted the Destruction of the World* || TB/1132

CHARLES Y. GLOCK & RODNEY STARK: Christian Beliefs and Anti-Semitism. *Introduction by the Authors* TB/1454

ALVIN W. GOULDNER: The Hellenic World TB/1479

ALVIN W. GOULDNER: Wildcat Strike: *A Study in Worker-Management Relationships* || TB/1176

CESAR GRANA: Modernity and Its Discontents: *French Society and the French Man of Letters in the Nineteenth Century* TB/1318

L. S. B. LEAKEY: Adam's Ancestors: *The Evolution of Man and His Culture. Illus.* TB/1019

KURT LEWIN: Field Theory in Social Science: *Selected Theoretical Papers.* || *Edited by Dorwin Cartwright* TB/1135

RITCHIE P. LOWRY: Who's Running This Town? *Community Leadership and Social Change* TB/1383

R. M. MACIVER: Social Causation TB/1153

GARY T. MARX: Protest and Prejudice: *A Study of Belief in the Black Community* TB/1435

ROBERT K. MERTON, LEONARD BROOM, LEONARD S. COTTRELL, JR., Editors: Sociology Today: *Problems and Prospects* ||
Vol. I TB/1173; Vol. II TB/1174

GILBERT OSOFSKY, Ed.: The Burden of Race: *A Documentary History of Negro-White Relations in America* TB/1405

GILBERT OSOFSKY: Harlem: The Making of a Ghetto: *Negro New York 1890-1930* TB/1381

TALCOTT PARSONS & EDWARD A. SHILS, Editors: Toward a General Theory of Action: *Theoretical Foundations for the Social Sciences* TB/1083

PHILIP RIEFF: The Triumph of the Therapeutic: *Uses of Faith After Freud* TB/1360

JOHN H. ROHRER & MUNRO S. EDMONSON, Eds.: The Eighth Generation Grows Up: *Cultures and Personalities of New Orleans Negroes* || TB/3050

ARNOLD ROSE: The Negro in America: *The Condensed Version of Gunnar Myrdal's An American Dilemma. Second Edition* TB/3048

GEORGE ROSEN: Madness in Society: *Chapters in the Historical Sociology of Mental Illness.* || *Preface by Benjamin Nelson* TB/1337

PHILIP SELZNICK: TVA and the Grass Roots: *A Study in the Sociology of Formal Organization* TB/1230

PITIRIM A. SOROKIN: Contemporary Sociological Theories: *Through the First Quarter of the Twentieth Century* TB/3046

MAURICE R. STEIN: The Eclipse of Community: *An Interpretation of American Studies* TB/1128

EDWARD A. TIRYAKIAN, Ed.: Sociological Theory, Values and Sociocultural Change: *Essays in Honor of Pitirim A. Sorokin* ° TB/1316

FERDINAND TONNIES: Community and Society: *Gemeinschaft und Gesellschaft. Translated and Edited by Charles P. Loomis* TB/1116

SAMUEL E. WALLACE: Skid Row as a Way of Life TB/1367

W. LLOYD WARNER: Social Class in America: *The Evaluation of Status* TB/1013

FLORIAN ZNANIECKI: The Social Role of the Man of Knowledge. *Introduction by Lewis A. Coser* TB/1372